The Houses of William Wurster

THE HOUSES OF
WILLIAM WURSTER
Frames for Living

Caitlin Lempres Brostrom and Richard C. Peters

Princeton Architectural Press · New York

Published by
Princeton Architectural Press
37 E 7th Street, New York, NY 10003

For a free catalog of books, call 1-800-722-6657
Visit our website at www.papress.com

Editor: Dan Simon
Designer: Paul Wagner

Special thanks to: Bree Anne Apperley, Sara Bader,
Nicola Bednarek Brower, Janet Behning, Fannie Bushin,
Megan Carey, Carina Cha, Tom Cho, Penny (Yuen Pik)
Chu, Russell Fernandez, Jan Haux, Jennifer Lippert,
John Myers, Katharine Myers, Margaret Rogalski,
Andrew Stepanian, Joseph Weston, and Deb Wood
of Princeton Architectural Press
—Kevin C. Lippert, publisher

Library of Congress
Cataloging-in-Publication Data

Brostrom, Caitlin Lempres.
The houses of William Wurster : frames for living /
Caitlin Lempres Brostrom and Richard C. Peters. —
1st ed.
    p.   cm.
Includes bibliographical references and index.
ISBN 978-1-61689-028-5 (alk. paper)
1. Wurster, William Wilson. 2. Architects—United
States—Biography. 3. Architecture, Domestic—
United States—History—20th century. I. Wurster,
William Wilson. II. Peters, Richard C. III. Title.
IV. Title: Frames for living.
NA737.W87B76 2011
720.92—dc22
[B]
                                    2010051195

CONTENTS

FOREWORD

Thinking back, an image that most endures in my mind is the white tower and compound of William Wurster's Warren Gregory House (1929) in the Santa Cruz Mountains. The Gregory Farmhouse, as it's usually referenced, is a misnomer: It is a country retreat designed and built between 1927 and 1929, a place of the soul, no doubt, for a very sophisticated San Francisco family.

The tower, slim and upright like a beacon suggests a reincarnation of the water towers still occasionally visible on Northern Californian farms. The tower anchors one corner of a beautifully simple, embracing composition, with two wings perpendicular to each other bracketing the opposite side of a tree-filled court. These wings are joined by a porch tucked under their eaves. The structures are beguilingly direct—yes, farmhouse direct—and narrow. They are mostly one-room wide, the roofs low and unprepossessing, the interiors made with very wide white-washed boards. Paned windows pace steadily across their sides and doors align strategically.

Photographs of the house made a singularly enchanting impression of the site, which I now realize was steeped in the most effective ways of forming memorable places: claiming place with a marker set upon the land, surrounding and giving shape to a calibrated set of rooms, both indoors and out, and investing them with thought and traces of a consistent sensibility applied to the ways in which things are made.

I no longer remember how that image came into my consciousness, I imagine it was probably in the 1950s, most likely through a book published by the Museum of Modern Art and owned by my father. However, it has never left me: it stays as the emblem of a place that could at once mark and embrace, be clear and gentle, determined and accommodating, joined to its surroundings and distinct. Such places give you something to stand beside, something to explore and be embraced by, and paths for the mind to follow.

The site plan drawing, which I only came to know later, has a great sweeping curved wall on the other side of the living spaces, creating a large, flat terrace on the sloping land, the gesture of a deft and knowing compositional hand. Like so many of Wurster's gestures, its sweep expands the outlook while hardly being apparent. Try it sometime: it's harder than it looks.

This book, which so richly reveals many of Wurster's fine houses, brings us back (or may we hope, forward?) to a milieu that valued accomplished modesty, spare spaces, and graceful movement; a period when to build directly and easily with materials close to hand was considered a virtue; one that would allow ingenuity to be invested in building arrangements that would embellish ways of living and being in a particular place.

The apparent ease of these buildings and the steady quiet confidence of Wurster's manner often veiled the reach of his intellect and the steely determination that together account for his powerful influence on the development of modern architecture. Steadfastly opposed to the doctrinaire, Wurster was not easily assimilated into the doctrinal confines of modern architecture, and was sometimes relegated to a position beyond the margins of Modernist discourse: An aberration at best, he certainly remained outside the International Style, which was then gaining preeminence. Yet the work of Wurster and others around him, especially the domestic work, was so clear, so evidently related to site and climate and direct ways of building, that it demanded respect, garnering a category of its own as the Bay Area Regional Style.

Nevertheless Wurster was always a force to be reckoned with. There he was at Harvard in 1943 (and commuting to Yale to teach) and at MIT as Dean of Architecture & Planning from 1944 to 1950, where he made significant transformations in the school's ethos. And there he was, from 1957–63 as a member of the Foreign Building Operations Advisory Group, overseeing the architecture of a wave of new U.S. embassy buildings, vigorously in keeping with the spirit of the times but in ways that were respectful of local traditions and places.

Returning to California in 1949 with his wife Catherine Bauer Wurster (herself a highly influential advocate for planning and housing), he became the Dean of Architecture at Berkeley. There he remade the school's structure and mission into the more encompassing College of Environmental Design, a move resisted by many in the American Institute of Architects (vainly), even mocked by some. The title has proven to be prescient. He and Catherine and their expanding circle of influential friends and colleagues laid a foundation for continuing growth and evolution in comprehension of the field.

A large part of Wurster's influence was carried forward by people for whom he opened and nurtured career paths. He had a great eye for talent. At MIT he appointed Lawrence Anderson as Department Head. Ralph Rapson, Vernon DeMars, and Kevin Lynch were appointed to the faculty during this period. Danish architectural writer Steen Eiler Ramussen and the great Finnish architect Alvar Aalto were visiting faculty. He was also instrumental in the appointment of Gyorgy Kepes as the leading figure in the visual arts there.

At Berkeley he forged the new college combining architecture, planning, and landscape architecture (and, a short-lived design department) into a confederation of departments that he peopled with a range of strong personages, complementing those already there and reaching into new territory.

One of the most telling characteristics of Bill Wurster's deanships was his commitment to creating opportunities for his faculty to do their own work. Not only did he insist that their professional work as architects was central to their academic effectiveness, but he also used his stature and persuasiveness to create opportunities for them within the university. Baker House dormitory at MIT was the most influential. It stands, still, as a primary example of Aalto's work in the U.S., a stunningly supple and pertinent urban addition to the Charles River frontage of MIT. Not far away is 100 Memorial Drive, an innovative apartment complex, still highly valued, which Wurster also arranged to have designed by a faculty team that included Ralph Rapson, Vernon DeMars, Robert Woods Kennedy, Carl Koch, and William Brown. At Berkeley the most prominent example is Wurster Hall, the building that houses the college, named in Bill and Catherine's honor. It too was designed with Wurster's patronage by a faculty team consisting of Joseph Esherick, Vernon DeMars, and Donald Olsen, an unlikely but fruitful gathering of talents and convictions.

A similar, but more personal assembly of talents and convictions took place higher on the hills in Berkeley, where Wurster (again linked with the Gregorys, who owned the land) arranged for the development of Greenwood Common, a collection of ten sites around a small common green, each to be designed by a notable architect from the Bay Area. Already on the site were houses by John Galen Howard, the seminal planner and architect of the Berkeley campus, and Rudolph Schindler, the fertile modern architect from Los Angeles. To these were added houses by Joseph Esherick, Donald Olsen, Marquis and Stoller, John Funk, Harwell Harris, and Henry Hill, and a landscape design by Lawrence Halprin.

As recounted by Waverly Lowell in her book *Living Modern: A Biography of Greenwood Common*, the property had been assembled by the Gregory family and its subsequent development was arranged and supervised by Wurster during the years 1952–57. From correspondence and interview recollections that she recounts, a sense of his quiet determination once again emerges, setting the general parameters for development, laying the ground work for thoughtful and mutually respectful work, and persuading clients of the benefits that will accrue to careful consideration of the whole, shaped around common space at the primary point of overlook to the bay. During the process, coming to live in the former Gregory house itself, Wurster presided (from a position slightly removed) over the harmonies and subtle melodies and very occasional dissonances being conducted.

Throughout, his sensibilities were fueled by his intellect and gave force to his authority. That he was so undemonstrative in manner seems to have been, in a curious way, a key to his exceptional strength and influence. His opinions were not given lightly. Nor were they likely to be superfluous. When rendered, they were resonant with authority. William Wurster did not push himself forward, rather he enabled the lives and works of others to flourish. Yet he was rigorous in attention to detail, astute in assessing and assembling appropriate levels of investment, and resolutely certain of the need for excellence, confident that in the design of environments, as in life, excellence could take many forms.

The book that follows allows an intense view, never before assembled in this way, into the genesis and enduring vitality of William Wurster's encounters with specific clients and sites, and the fine buildings that resulted. It draws from insights and personal understanding of Wurster and his works that Richard Peters garnered over decades as a friend and as faculty at Berkeley, and from the documents and original photographs entrusted to him. These have been wonderfully supplemented by the research, writings, and photographs of current conditions that Caitlin Lempres Brostrom brings to the project, along with an intense dedication to bringing it all together in proper form. *The Houses of William Wurster* sets another Wurster landmark within the culture of our times.

Donlyn Lyndon, FAIA, Topaz Medalist DPACSA, Eva Li Professor Emeritus of Architecture and Urban Design College of Environmental Design, University of California, Berkeley

William Wurster in the 1960s as dean at the College of Environmental Design at the University of California, Berkeley

PREFACE

We embarked on this book knowing that William Wurster was a larger-than-life figure. He affected innumerable people through the enjoyment of his architecture (over 2,000 projects, with over 1,300 residential commissions), his influence on education, and his powerful ability to shape and direct other professionals. It was a daunting prospect to describe his multifaceted life and discuss and display the quality of his architectural designs in meaningful depth. We first thought to limit the book to the work from his architectural office before World War II and the formation of his partnership with Theodore Bernardi and Donn Emmons (the legacy of Wurster and his talented partners is worthy of an in-depth study of its own). It became clear that attempting to document all of Wurster's work over his fifty-year career would give none of it the justice and understanding it deserves.

The necessary and extremely helpful limitations of publishing, and reality, quickly narrowed our scope to Wurster's houses. It is here that his brilliance, innovation, and influence is most evident, and through the lens of this one architectural genre we could chronicle, with carefully selected examples, the span of his career.

Houses are personal, and each of us has a particular relationship to the spaces we inhabit. Wurster truly understood this and he applied his considerable talent to creating homes that reflected and expanded his clients' lives. He had a unique ability to arrange rooms with generous daylight while capturing the qualities of the surrounding landscape and environment, all with an unmatched elegance taken from everyday materials and details. Ultimately, the beautiful spaces in his houses affect their occupants every day.

Wurster felt it was important not to demand the "scraping of knuckles" of the client with the arbitrary design decisions of the architect.[1] His intention was to create a place that allowed life to unfold naturally, to be what Wurster often called, "a frame for living." Wurster used this phrase in contrast to "machines for living," as other architects chose to ascribe to describe how houses should be designed; it was always present in our minds as we worked, and it became the frame for this book.

We selected thirty-three houses out of Wurster's residential commissions. The choice was difficult because many favorites had to be passed over. To follow the arc of his architectural brilliance we have included houses that have been published before, in addition to houses new to public exposure; there are houses that Wurster was particularly fond of and houses that illustrate his core design intentions, and all are historically important in the development of his career. The houses also represent a variety of responses to mountain, city, suburban, and seashore environments, and they date from the 1920s to the 1960s. There are so many of his houses, equally well designed, that are not shown and many stories still untold.

The completion of this work has taken us much longer than we could have imagined. And yet, it does seem that the best time for this book is now: the renewed appreciation for architecture that is authentic, appropriate, and modest will carry Wurster's work into this century. Over the intervening years, thousands of documents, drawings, and photographs have been catalogued and digitized in the Wurster collection at the Environmental Design Archives, allowing students, teachers, architects, planners, and everyone else a first-hand look at his ingenious work and design brilliance.

Graciously, many of the current owners of Wurster's houses allowed us access to their homes; some of these houses are lovingly tended in their original state while others have been renewed in ways that accentuate the clarity of their architecture. The residents of these houses were all enthusiastic about this book. Their interest was particularly piqued after hearing the book's title: they all, without a doubt, have never lived in a house that was a more perfect frame for their lives than the one Wurster designed.

———

In 1958, William Wurster invited Richard Peters to teach in the Department of Architecture at Berkeley. Peters had just graduated from Princeton and Wurster, like he had with so many others in his life, took a personal interest in Peters' career both as a teacher and an architect. Peters' architectural interests are in day lighting, which began as a graduate student, and he was encouraged by Wurster to develop courses at Berkeley that focused on this aspect of architectural design. When it came time for Peters' sabbatical, after expressing interest in understanding the extremes of daylight and its affect on architecture, Wurster arranged a trip to Finland and a meeting with his personal friend, the architect Alvar Aalto. Peters' studies of Aalto's masterful architecture revealed the inseparable relationship between daylighting and electric lighting, and it become a major factor in Peters' teaching, architectural work, and soon the buildings of many of his closest architectural friends.

Peters lived in an apartment close by the Wurster family and he was often invited to "fill in" at Friday night dinners with Wurster's wife, Catherine, and notable friends and dignitaries. Peters learned how deeply Wurster cared and nurtured the people in his life, family, colleagues, and his clients. By 1963 Wurster was diagnosed with Parkinson's disease and Peters would drive Bill (as he insisted everyone call him) and Ernesto Rogers (Italian architect and visiting professor) to visit his former projects—especially his houses. It was Wurster's insights from these small tours that became Peters' inspiration for sharing Wurster's architecture. Rogers asked Peters to write an article on Wurster for the Italian journal *Casabella*, and in 1964 Catherine Wurster asked Peters to consider writing a book about her husband: he began this project soon after.

After Wurster died in 1973, Bernardi and Emmons wanted to clean out old office files, intending to discard the papers from before their partnership's formation in the early 1940s. Peters offered to take the files, and the multiple boxes were delivered to his small campus office. Until his retirement in 1994, Peters continued to teach full time, maintain an active role in the development of the university campus, practice architecture, and find time to write several periodical articles about Wurster's life and architecture. He worked on the book concurrently, transcribing many of the loose papers and journals and interviewing as many people as possible who knew Wurster. In 1991, Peters asked his former graduate student, Caitlin (neé King) Lempres Brostrom to take on the completion of the book.

Lempres Brostrom was born while Peters was a young faculty member at Berkeley. Both her parents had been students at the school, study-ing in the architecture program run by Wurster. Her father worked for Wurster after finishing his degree and she has distinct memories of the two of them in his office at the old brick Icehouse near the San Francisco wharf. Her father received an interdisciplinary PhD at Berkeley, her mother, a professor, wrote about architecture and taught design at Berkeley and in Norway until she retired in 2000. Lempres Brostrom was brought up in a family deeply entrenched in the love of archi-tecture, and with its constant discussion and evaluation. Growing up in the San Francisco Bay Area, she was surrounded by Wurster's architecture.

In 1987, while a graduate architectural design student, she began working in the Environmental Design Archives (then, the Documents Collection) at Berkeley's College of Environmental Design. She soon began to fully appreciate the lessons that could be learned by studying the original design documents of gifted architects. One of her responsibilities was to work with the Wurster documents that Peters was pass-ing onto the archive. With this rare opportunity to study his design methodology through letters, drawings, and photographs, she was reawakened to the genius of Wurster's work in the context of the era he worked in. She used the knowledge about appropriateness and responsiveness to site and client to help build her own successful private practice after graduation. She was delighted to accept Peters' request to bring this book to completion.

1. William Wurster, early 1940s

2. Coleman House, hall, atrium, with view to living room and San Francisco Bay

A PROFESSIONAL LIFE 1917–1973

"The frame for living is life itself, so do the thing which leaves room for the growth of the occupant without his scraping his knuckles against your arbitrary decisions with each change in his development."[1]

William Wilson Wurster sensed unique qualities in the geography and social fabric of the San Francisco Bay Area and its environs, and as a native of the region, he was particularly compelled to convey its character in his architecture. [FIG. 1] Wurster's regional emphasis was similar to the general concerns of thoughtful architects everywhere: features of site and climate, and the personal needs of the client must inform the design approach. Yet Wurster's singular interpretation of these considerations distinguished him from his contemporaries. His formal training combined with his rural upbringing and the expansive possibilities of the twentieth century shaped a style of architecture that is distinctly Californian.

Wurster solved architectural problems with quiet, understated elegance. He became intimately involved with his client's desires, and their homes and offices were a response to his understanding of their needs, and perhaps more than anything, to the way people lived in California. He imbued very simple things with gracefulness, approaching a window detail with as much care as a primary living space. His rooms didn't rely on formal geometry or style, and if there was a consistent element in his work it was simplicity; to paraphrase his wife and noted planner Catherine Bauer Wurster, it didn't make any difference what a project cost, it would never show. [FIG. 2]

Although many of Wurster's projects are considered modern architecture, this was not due to any conscious determination of style on his part. Wurster's goal was always to interpret his client's desires in a simple and elegant way. His houses required only the most basic construction methods, and they didn't demand unusual skills; their refinement relied on a deep, practical knowledge of building that was passed along from carpenter to carpenter. Wurster's sensibilities dovetailed perfectly with this style of building: he was able to pay attention to the smallest of details, yet never had to compromise his vision nor that of his client. And because building traditions varied from region to region, he customized each project to fit the particulars of the site and blend faultlessly with the surrounding terrain. Studying Wurster's work, especially his houses, over his forty years of practice presents a rare opportunity to explore his tremendous breadth of design elements and follow his development as an architect.

When Wurster started out, like most young architects in the 1920s, his first houses were designed in the prevalent traditional styles reminiscent of England, France, and the Mediterranean. Even then, he was certain of his goals, as evidenced by the similarity of his architectural language in his later modern work. He remained steadfastly and ingeniously true to his overall vision of ideal California living, and his later work displayed both high sophistication and reasoned austerity.

Wurster had the audacity to panel elegantly scaled living rooms for wealthy families in re-sawn, whitewashed redwood planks. He gave halls, porches, and breezeways greater scale and importance as primary living and transitional spaces between inside and outside. As early as the mid 1920s, Wurster set the stage and then

3. Sullivan House living porch, Saratoga, California, 1939

directed the development of a relaxed modernist style of wood construction. Clients appreciated his approach, proven by the national attention he received in the decade following as his work came to mirror their Depression-era sensibilities of living comfortably without obvious ostentation. He not only took advantage of regional materials, but gave their use a much broader integrity. For every architect striving to design with a sensitivity to materials—as so many are in contemporary practice—Wurster's work provides endless insight.

From 1927 to 1942, the years of his independent practice, Wurster designed more than two hundred houses (a fraction of his over 1,300 residential commissions). He became the recognized leader of a group of young San Francisco Bay Area architects whose work, especially in residential design, made significant contributions to mid-twentieth-century American architecture. In 1942, Wurster's private practice expanded, first with Theodore Bernardi and, later, Donn Emmons as partners, and he continued to design private homes. After World War II the primary focus of their office shifted toward urban planning and large commercial construction. Concurrently, Wurster revamped the architectural schools at MIT (1945–50) and at the University of California, Berkeley (1951–63). As dean in both of these large institutional settings, he influenced architectural education significantly in the United States.

Regardless of the scope of Wurster's efforts—whether a small farmhouse or a large urban mixed-use complex with multiple associated architects—his work, above all, reflects a sense of appropriateness to the period, the site, and the climate. Wurster's practice was primarily in Northern and Central California, which encompasses a wide variety of climates and terrain. This diversity encouraged Wurster to create many distinctive indoor-outdoor architectural relationships. The region's dry summers and temperate winters are conducive to outdoor living spaces; in the scorching Central Valley his designs tamed the sun, while in San Francisco's coastal fog his plans made optimal use of the available warmth and light.

Wurster's contributions to domestic architecture are so subtly integrated into this context that the casual eye often misses them. His houses appear to be of no distinctive style and were typically built with readily available materials and standard construction details. A lingering eye, however, quickly notices the subtlety of Wurster's palette, his unique sense of scale, and his extraordinary skill in integrating each building within its site and taking full advantage of the environmental opportunities. To paraphrase Wurster: his houses were designed to be the frame for living, not the picture.[2]

Rather than balancing one style against another and selecting the best solutions of his predecessors, Wurster refined early California colonial and vernacular elements and adapted them to contemporary situations in innovative

4. Architecture faculty and students, University of California, Berkeley, ca. 1918. Front row, instructors from left, Warren Perry, John Galen Howard, and William Hayes; rear, students from left, G.J. Fitzgerald, Lionel Pries, Eldridge Spencer, D. Lovell, and M. Gunzdorfer

ways. His earliest summer houses often appear to be a collection of barely connected buildings, an approach that maximized the advantages of the site and the access to natural light in every room while minimizing disturbance of the surroundings. Wurster's true genius as an architectural interpreter of modern life shows itself in the way he connected the traditional spaces of a house. He gave staircases, halls, porches, and breezeways greater scale and importance as living and transitional spaces between inside and outside, frequently incorporating exterior details—brick pavers and rough-sawn siding, for example—into interior spaces, which he then described as "living porches," "kitchen caves," and "rooms with no name." Wurster's ingenuity and regional attunement generated a series of innovations that have enriched American architecture immensely. [FIG. 3]

————

William Wilson Wurster, the son of Fredrick and Maude Wurster, was born on October 20, 1895, in the San Joaquin Valley town of Stockton, California. His family was large and well-connected to established California families, who later helped to establish Wurster. Within his family, Wilson (as he was called in his youth) learned early on how to relate comfortably to an intellectually and financially prominent group of people. These early-learned skills were essential to his ability to cultivate his broad and socially influential clientele.[3]

Wurster's early life was directed by a dedicated family who stressed the importance of his education. His father, a banker with frequent holidays, took him to see the inner workings of a steel foundry, the firehouse, and printing and tax collector's offices because he wanted William to know "how things worked."[4] His mother taught him the values of reading, observing, and describing places, people, and events. He exhibited a precocious interest in architecture; at the age of four, during the construction of his family's home, he inquired "How do chimneys stick on these steep roofs?"[5] As a boy, young Wurster was able to draw any house in town completely from memory, and while in high school he worked for the well-known Stockton architect E. B. Brown, taking measurements, drawing plans, and making blueprints. He never doubted that architecture was his vocation.

In 1913, Wurster enrolled in the University of California, Berkeley, to study architecture in the school's four-year program. That same year John Galen Howard arrived to administer the construction of the new campus and to head the architecture school, where he promptly instituted the École des Beaux-Arts method of instruction. Wurster received the highest marks for his engineering courses, but he was less successful in producing the beautiful drawings emblematic of the Beaux-Arts tradition. [FIGS. 4–6] He did not study with Howard directly, but the classical spirit that Howard revered molded his education. Wurster

5. Jane K. Sather Tower,
watercolor by
John Galen Howard

6. Hearst Mining Building, University of California, Berkeley,
sketch by John Galen Howard

joined the Sigma Chi fraternity, which was significant in the early development of his practice, as well as to the development of his character. Wurster once said his fraternity brothers helped him to become less opinionated in his expression, blunting his edges.[6]

Wurster greatly admired the architecture of the Craftsman era and studied many of the early Craftsman houses in Berkeley and San Francisco. In addition to Howard, his early education also exposed him to the work of Willis Polk, Ernest Coxhead, Louis Christian Mullgardt, Bernard Maybeck, Julia Morgan, Charles and Henry Greene, William Charles Hays, and Warren Perry. Hays and Perry (who was director of Berkeley's architecture department for thirty-four years), taught Wurster at Berkeley.

In 1915, Wurster contracted typhoid fever, which interrupted his studies and prevented him from joining the navy during World War I. He instead took marine engineering and ship design courses at Berkeley and joined the merchant marine for six months. He then returned to the architecture department, graduating with honors in June 1919.

After graduation, Wurster briefly worked for San Francisco architect John Reid Jr., at whose firm he learned drafting, devoting most of his time to plans for San Francisco schools, including Galileo High School. In May 1920, he became the architectural designer for Charles Dean, an architect on the staff of the Filtration Division of the City of Sacramento. Wurster prepared the working drawings of Dean's design for a new filtration

plant for the city of Sacramento and supervised the construction until its completion in 1922.

His involvement in multiple aspects of the project gave Wurster valuable practical experience and allowed him to understand and carefully document each phase of construction. Chester Gillespie, the chief filtration engineer and a professor at Berkeley while Wurster was a student, became an early client. Wurster built a cottage in Oakland hills for him in 1925; it was Wurster's earliest example of using local building customs and materials to build a home that was a "regional" response—a seed for his future work.

Taking advantage of his new-found freedom from academic life, Wurster continued his field study of buildings with Edward L. Barnett, a draftsman in the Dean office during the 1920s. They went on sketching trips to Monterey to see the Casa Ameste and the Larkin house, and to San Juan Bautista to sketch the mission and its auxiliary structures. Barnett said that he and Wurster also perused the Dean library, paying particular attention to books on Spanish architecture because of the region's similarity to that of California.[7]

From 1920 to 1922, while working on the filtration plant, Wurster moonlighted on a few residences. Most were similar to those published in the current trade journals but with differences that reflected the region. The very careful relationships that Wurster was later to expound—straightforward plans only loosely linked to traditional formal arrangements; the use of simple materials to produce plain, unadorned surfaces; windows arranged to suit the view and solar orientation; minimizing

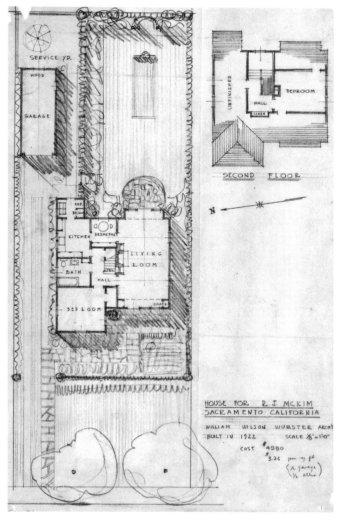

7. Floor plan, R.J. McKim House, ca. 1922

8. R.J. McKim House, ca. 1922

9. William Wurster, 1920s

certain traditional spaces allowing preserved spaces to expand, making small houses seem much larger than they were; and the orientation of gracious living spaces toward landscaped garden spaces were part of his architectural vocabulary even then. [FIGS.7+8]

In April 1922, Wurster applied for his Architectural Certificate. He included in the application work done while a student at Berkeley, the Sacramento Filtration Plant, and houses for the Breuner, McKim, and Grunsky families. John Galen Howard endorsed his application, as did Warren Perry, Charles K. Summer, William Hays, and Charles Dean. When Wurster appeared before the board they told him that he had the best-documented application they had ever

considered. He became a registered architect in California at the age of twenty-seven.

In May 1922, having saved four-thousand dollars, Wurster began an architectural Grand Tour of Europe to complete his classical education. [FIG.9] He kept a daily travel diary documenting his impressions of monuments, buildings, and scenic sites; he sketched and measured some, but found deeper understanding by studying the social context of what he saw. Wurster asserted, "It changed my whole point of view from one of eclectic skill to much more an attempt at fundamental knowledge."[8] Wurster's world was enlarged intellectually, socially, and architecturally during this trip. Two classmates from Berkeley, Eldridge ("Ted") and Jeanette Spencer, students at the

École des Beaux-Arts and the Louvre, introduced him to other American academics, many of whom were architects who later became leading teachers in their discipline.

Wurster's travels exposed him to works of art and architecture he had known only through such texts as Banister Fletcher's *A History of Architecture*. He explored Villa d'Este in Tivoli and its legendary gardens—a masterpiece of architecture and landscape design mentioned in Fletcher's tome, now a UNESCO World Heritage Site—and said of them: "I am filled with awe at the wonders of man's planning when combined with nature's creations. This tying together of the works of man and nature is a noble thing and here is the place to study it."[9] Yet he learned much from ordinary buildings as well: "Every little shack has more architecture per square inch than some of our good work. There seems to be a dignity about window and door openings which we do not possess. They always have the strong vertical feeling....The rural architecture all seems to suit the place, the climate, and the way of life of the people."[10]

His travels in Italy also brought him to Vicenza, where he studied and drew the buildings of Andrea Palladio. Wurster made particularly prescient observations in terms of the direction of his own architecture. He made particular note of the farm buildings, especially "the joining of a sort of wagon shed to the house...it would make such a fine airy porch at home." He again expressed admiration for humble but well-conceived structures, "...in these simple buildings lies our solution, and not in the intricate Gothic or ornate Renaissance. In a word, the beauty should come in a study of proportions and not mere application of forms to re-create."[11]

Wurster traveled throughout England, touring the planned towns of Letchworth and Welwyn with their designer, the British urban planner Ebenezer Howard, and learning about his garden cities. At the turn of the nineteenth century, a mass exodus from the English countryside resulted in overcrowded cities and unbearable conditions. Howard developed his garden city, which combined sunlight and gardens with the amenities of cities, as a way to return displaced agricultural workers to the countryside.[12] Wurster said that this European experience, and in particular his tour with Howard, made a great impression on him.

Wurster returned to New York in May 1923 with the intention of working for the renowned firm of McKim, Mead & White (where his mentor John Galen Howard had once worked). But on the advice of Shelley Morgan, a Princeton professor whom Wurster met in Europe, and of his former teacher William Hays, he was instead introduced to William Adams Delano and Chester Holmes Aldrich. In June 1923, Wurster started work as a draftsman at the well-regarded New York firm of Delano and Aldrich, designers of the Rockefeller estate in Westchester County, the Otto Kahn chateau in Cold Spring Harbor, the J. A. Burden house at Syosset, as well as many other residences for prominent families.

At the time, draftsmen rarely visited the buildings they were working on. Ignoring convention, Wurster organized trips—which Delano wholeheartedly endorsed and helped to arrange—of clubs, schools, and the dwellings of wealthy clients. Wurster was encouraged to continue his studies, and he competed in the Beaux-Arts Institute program in New York City, working in the famous New York atelier of George Licht, whom he had met traveling in Europe. There, studying alongside Louis I. Kahn, he won the Second Medal for the design of an office building in New York (Kahn won first prize).

Delano and Aldrich intentionally kept their office small so they could personally review the work of all their draftsmen, and they structured it as a system of ateliers or teams, the model Wurster later employed in his own office. One of Wurster's first assignments was to render plans for the book, *Portrait of Ten Country Houses Designed by Delano and Aldrich*. The project gave him the opportunity to visit each house with Delano and learn firsthand how the houses and their accompanying grounds and gardens were designed. Studying these houses in their settings gave Wurster a greater awareness of the relation of buildings to landscape, and formed the basis for his later principles of outdoor space in architecture, an integral element of his design repertoire. Wurster developed a lifelong friendship with

10. Oyster Bay Dutch Reformed Church, Brookville, Long Island, 1924

Delano and spent the summer of 1924 with the family in Syosset on Long Island. There, he tutored Delano's son Richard and experienced a very different lifestyle than he had previously known.

His apprenticeship in the Delano office included a variety of jobs: making measured drawings for additions to Long Island estates, tracing plans and inking final presentation drawings, developing sketches that Delano drew on the commuter train from Long Island to New York City, and even designing light fixtures. In addition to this general work, Wurster worked on three principal projects: The Round Hill Country Club in Greenwich, Connecticut, the Music School for the Sacred Heart Convent in New York, and the Oyster Bay Dutch Reformed Church in Brookville on Long Island (also known as the Brookville Church), which he designed in 1924 during his summer stay with the Delanos. [FIG. 10]

Wurster and Delano corresponded for many years, and Delano's letters were always encouraging and filled with admiration for Wurster's buildings and his success. Much later, in February 1937, Delano wrote: "The copy of the Forum which reproduced some pictures of your houses [Donald

Gregory, Robbins, Voss, Benner], leads me to think that you are very much on the right track. The houses all have charm and are good, straightforward solutions to the problems involved. It makes me very proud to think that some of the skill which you display may have been acquired in this office."[13]

In August 1924, Charles G. Hyde, chief sanitary engineer in California and a professor at the University of California, Berkeley, offered Wurster the opportunity to design the Upper San Leandro Filtration Plant for the East Bay Water Company. Wurster left the office of Delano and Aldrich and returned to California in September to begin work on the project, which was completed in 1926. Thanks to a loan from Delano upon his departure from the firm, Wurster opened his small practice in 1924 in Berkeley's Hotel Whitecotton, which became his base for the filtration plant design as well as for other projects.

One month after he had returned to Berkeley, Wurster received a letter from Delano telling of a potential commission from his friend Elizabeth Ellis, a socially prominent woman from Long Island who maintained a house in the milder climate of

Berkeley because of her son's chronic asthma. Ellis' home on Ridge Road was a haven for artists and intellectuals; she gave weekly dinners to introduce new people of interest to each other. After meeting Ellis in October, Wurster attended many of these dinners and there met many of his future clients. She remained his patron until her death in 1959.

Through Elizabeth Ellis, Wurster met Sarah and Warren Gregory, a family who lived nearby in a Berkeley hills house (designed by John Galen Howard in 1904). It was a wooded retreat and a center of social life in Berkeley. Sarah Gregory, the matriarch of Berkeley society, recommended Wurster's services to many in her circle. These two gifted and influential women, Ellis and Gregory, provided a great impetus to Wurster's career, both by the work he did for them and the introductions he received through them.

Life in the Bay Area was prosperous in the mid 1920s and building activity flourished. Wurster's houses from this period took advantage of the temperate climate and indigenous materials, and although the houses were designed in various modified styles, they responded to their clients' needs and made the most of their sites.

At this point, Wurster was not consciously involved in any derivative California style, but approached each project individually. Wurster's house designs largely depended on what he thought was appropriate and, based on common sense, clients usually accepted his judgments. Many of his details or spatial concepts appeared more modern than the traditional "stylistic" approach encouraged by trade journals and general architectural practice, but it was not until the 1934 Frederic Benner house that Wurster became interested in modernism as an expressed style, and only then because the client requested it. Wurster's architectural vocabulary began to shift from a perceptive yet mainstream approach as seen in his earliest projects (see Kellam, Smith, Hagar) where he used referential architectural details but minimized them as far as he dared and his clients allowed. He also began to explore using carpenter-style architecture derived from vernacular California building details—as seen in the Gillespie house—which became a signature

style that set the tone for much of his initial award-winning work.

Wurster's diaries from this time typically mention places and buildings that influenced him. His noticeable lack of reference to any knowledge or interest in schools of architectural thought is significant considering the number of contemporary trade publications that included the works of international architects, such as those later associated with the Bauhaus. This disinterest is partly understandable in light of his own classical background, his Beaux-Arts education, his apprenticeship in the traditional firm of Delano and Aldrich, and his practice in Northern California, which developed an architecture of its own under such leaders as Willis Polk, Julia Morgan, Bernard Maybeck, Arthur Brown, and John Galen Howard. On a trip to Southern California in July 1926 (primarily to look at churches in Santa Barbara, Los Angeles, and San Diego), one cannot help but notice that Wurster made no comments in his diary about the works of Frank Lloyd Wright, Richard Neutra, Rudolf Schindler, or Irving Gill.

Wurster was entertained in Spanish Colonial Revival homes in Montecito designed by the renowned George Washington Smith and was impressed by their response to the warm climate, as they seamlessly integrated house and garden and afforded a gracious lifestyle. He came to Santa Barbara to visit with his friends from college, Elizabeth and Lockwood deForest. Lockwood deForest and Wurster met their last year (1919) at Berkeley while deForest was studying landscape architecture. Partly because of their friendship, but also because Elizabeth's parents knew William Delano, deForest's in-laws (the Frederick Kellam family) hired Wurster and deForest to design a house in 1928 (see pages 46–49). At the same time they collaborated on Mr. and Mrs. Gerald Hagar's home in the Berkeley hills. Wurster and deForest went on to design at least ten projects together over the next decade; along with Elizabeth deForest and Thomas and Elizabeth Church, the five were close friends.

In 1926, after living in and remodeling Ellis's Ridge Street house while the family summered on Long Island, Wurster relocated his office to the Newhall Building (260 California Street) in San

11. W. Gregory House, 1928

Francisco. Employing a single draftsperson, he began the design work for the First Congregational Church in Stockton, the church that his family attended and where his parents were married.

Wurster continued to explore style as it related to a building's function in the houses he designed until 1929. It was not until Wurster's project in the Santa Cruz Mountains for the Gregory family that his work truly expressed the feeling of place and time; it was his first project in a new signature idiom that was both ingenious and appropriate. Some of its elements could be seen earlier on but this project explored new ideas throughout. The Gregory farmhouse (1927–29), an unadorned whitewashed redwood structure, had its roots in the vernacular tradition of carpenter building in California. The influence of this house at the time, and especially after it was awarded *House Beautiful*'s first prize a few years later, established Wurster as a West Coast architect of national interest. [FIG. 11]

Wurster's practice expanded dramatically in the 1930s beginning with a series of commissions by the internationally famous golfer Marion Hollins to design her house and other residences and structures at the 600-plus acre Pasatiempo Country Club and Estates near the Santa Cruz Mountains. Hollins had just completed the enormously successful Cypress Point golf course at Pebble Beach at nearby Monterey Bay. Using $2.5 million of her own money, Marion Hollins wanted to create her own community that combined a world-class golf course with equal equestrian facilities. Renowned designer Dr. Alister Mackenzie laid out the course while the Olmstead Brothers provided

the landscaping for the course and general grounds. Wurster was introduced to Hollins in late 1928 by Elizabeth Ellis. Initially Hollins felt the architecture should be "rather English in character, as the property is covered with beautiful oaks."[14] Hollins and her general manager, Earle Howes, were exposed specifically to the nearby Gregory farmhouse by Wurster as an example of what he felt was appropriate for the architecture of this new community. Hollins ultimately hired the well-established architect, Clarence Tantau, to design the clubhouse and Wurster to design "all the other buildings."[15] Wurster introduced Marion Hollins to the then-relatively unknown landscape architect Thomas Church, who oversaw the landscaping work in relation to the various structures.

Tantau, Wurster, and Church became the architectural advisory board for all projects within the development. Wurster designed Hollins' own home as well as others for her family and the staff (see General Manager's, Church). Additionally, he designed many of the support facilities: the caddy house, the tennis courts, a bath house at the beach (never built), the swimming pool, and nearby stables in Scott's Valley. Unfortunately, the opening of the community coincided with the collapse of the stock market in October 1929 and the beginning of the Great Depression. Nonetheless, Wurster did build several additional private homes in Pasatiempo (see Berry/Lombardi, Butler) through the late 1930s—most of his projects there received numerous national and local awards and were thoroughly published by trade and consumer magazines. Despite the success for Wurster, the development suffered from the effects of the

12. Alvar Aalto's home, 1937

13. Thomas Church, Elizabeth Church, Aino Aalto, and
William Wurster, 1937

Depression. Hollins sold her interest and moved back to Monterey in the late 1930s.

Despite the economic restrictions of the time, Wurster's architecture, which relied on simple, local materials and details, represented a portfolio of work that clearly delineated him as an architect of established national reputation. Almost all of these structures, despite being clearly regional in language, were awarded numerous national awards and were published in all of the national design and mainstream journals. Wurster presented a very appealing aesthetic to a country trying to recover from the excesses of the 1920s and the ravages of the Great Depression that followed.

Partially as a result of his work at Pasatiempo, Wurster designed many other homes during this time. At Pasatiempo and elsewhere, his methods of construction, while not new, continued to be innovative and trendsetting in their application. His new use of old principles and of carpenter-simple plans and details resulted in houses reminiscent of traditional domestic spaces and yet fit a more modern life. The majority of Wurster's projects during this period were situated in rural settings and were intended for summer use.[16]

The ability to live both inside and out without a clear transition in the quality of the spaces was well suited to Wurster's evolving architecture language. He continued to explore using easily available and inexpensive materials and detailing in the design of homes focused on responding to the specifics of their environment: from the hot summers of the Central Valley to the punishing waves along the San Francisco Bay shoreline.

Wurster developed designs that felt straightforward and unforced in their solution but which felt inherently unique in how they captured views and natural light and created sheltered spaces (see Sloss, Voss, Benner, Kenyon, Dondo, Jenson, and Chickering).

In 1937, Wurster joined Thomas and Elizabeth Church on a trip to northern Europe. Wurster's work had at this point been published in Europe, most notably in the German magazine *Moderne Bauformen*. The three traveled as inexpensively as possible, riding third-class on the Challenger train across the U.S. to New York, sailing third class on the Cunard Line to England and on to Scandinavia. In England they saw Berthold Lubetkin's magnificent Penguin Pool at the Regents Park Zoo—built in 1933, its taut interlacing ramps lent an abstract sculptural quality. As guests of Kay Fisker in Denmark, they toured his houses in Copenhagen, they saw social housing projects in Sweden, and visited Gunnar Asplund's concert hall in Göteberg. While in Sweden they were encouraged by the architects they met to continue on to Finland to see the new architecture there.

It was a fortuitous trip and they had many encounters with Finnish architects. [FIGS. 12–14] The most thrilling of these was their chance meeting with Alvar Aalto. On a drive through the outskirts of Helsinki, they spotted a remarkable house, and Wurster, wanting to know who designed it, rang the doorbell. It was Aalto's design and Aalto's house. "We had Rhine wine and coffee, and the next hour we had Rhine wine and coffee, and the third hour we had Rhine wine and coffee.... And thus began a

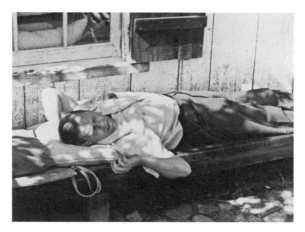

14. Elizabeth Church, William Wurster, and Alvar Aalto, in Aalto's home, 1937

15. Alvar Aalto at the Gregory Farmhouse, 1939

16. Staff of the Wurster office, left to right: William Wurster, Theodore Bernardi, Alfred Day, William Rice, Robert Deshon, Arne Kartwold, Joseph Johnson, Frederick Langhorst, Flloyd Comstock, Donn Emmons, and Fred B. Barss

17. Catherine Bauer at about the time of her marriage to Wurster in 1940

fabulous friendship."[17] The trio traveled through Paris on their way home and saw Aalto's Finnish Pavilion at the World's Fair. Of Aalto's work, Wurster later said, "I don't believe in having gods in architecture because I think we all have frailties as human beings, but [Aalto] is a person more thoughtful than most, driving on in his quiet way, never ceasing to flow."[18] Two years later Aalto traveled to San Francisco to see the 1939 Golden Gate International Exposition, which included Wurster's Yerba Buena Women's Clubhouse. Their friendship was steady for the rest of their lives with numerous visits and professional exchanges. [FIG. 15]

After his travels to Europe and until the war years of the 1940s, Wurster refined his approach to the resolution of issues regarding client needs, economics, site, and climate. The resulting work appears even simpler and more direct in form than his earlier houses and are less obviously regional in their exterior expression (see Miller, Hamill, Mendenhall, Clark, Green, Gerbode, Wolski). In fact, some of these prewar projects appear to be sleek and nearly modern in the traditional sense. These were the last houses that Wurster designed before the formation of his partnership with Theodore Bernardi. [FIG. 16]

In 1940, Wurster met Catherine Bauer while she was teaching at Berkeley.[19] [FIG. 17] The two of them were married after a six-month courtship. Bauer was a planner and the author of the seminal book *Modern Housing* (1934), who that same year held the Rosenburg Lectureship in the School of

19. Donn Emmons and Theodore Bernardi as partners with Wurster after his return to California in 1950

18. War housing, Vallejo, California, 1943

Social Welfare at the University of California, Berkeley. A protégé of the noted East Coast writer and planner Lewis Mumford, Catherine was instrumental in drafting the landmark 1937 U.S. Housing Act, the first to provide for federally subsidized housing. She was a key figure in a small idealistic and influential group of people who called themselves "housers" because of their commitment to improving housing for low-income families. With Mumford's encouragement, Bauer had traveled throughout Europe in the late 1920s and developed strong friendships with key postwar architects interested in change including Ernst May, André Lurçat, and Walter Gropius. Bauer and her colleagues dramatically changed the concept of social housing in the United States and inspired a generation of urban activists to integrate public housing into the emerging welfare state of the mid twentieth century. During her life, Bauer advised five presidents on the development of national social housing policy. Bauer-Wurster was a professor of urban and city planning at UC Berkeley for the rest of her life.[20]

In 1943, after completing 5,000 units of war worker housing with the architect Ernest Kump in Vallejo, California, at the urging of his wife, Wurster took some time off and accepted a Wheelwright Fellowship to study at Harvard University. [FIG. 18] "I didn't just want to go on being a successful

architect, but I wanted to get an insight into Catherine's world."[21] The couple moved to Cambridge, Massachusetts, and Wurster began studying toward a doctorate in planning under John M. Gaus, professor of government at Harvard and a scholar in the field of regional planning. Around the same time Wurster was also asked to teach at Yale's School of Fine Arts. In 1944, after a year at Harvard, James Killian, President of MIT, with the encouragement of Professor Lawrence Anderson, invited Wurster to become dean of the School of Architecture and Planning. To maintain his West Coast office, Wurster converted his individual practice into a partnership with his longtime associate Theodore Bernardi. Although the firm continued to design private residences, its focus shifted because of World War II. In addition to commercial projects, the firm began developing war-housing complexes in partnership with Ernest Kump and others. Despite his East Coast duties, Wurster remained involved in his California office through a constant coast-to-coast exchange of drawings. Primarily, though, Wurster committed himself to reorganizing the architectural program at MIT. He did not design projects in the Boston area because he felt he was not familiar enough with the region and lifestyle.

While Wurster was at MIT, he and Bernardi expanded their partnership with the addition of Donn Emmons in 1945. [FIG. 19] Wurster, Bernardi & Emmons flourished and became a training ground for generations of architects. Wurster insisted that the firm provide the younger architects with the full gamut of architectural experiences rather than assigning limited, repetitive tasks. Similarly, the practice never deliberately specialized but accepted design jobs ranging from kitchen remodels to international bank headquarters. As at Delano and Aldrich, jobs were organized around teams. Wurster explained, "Team members rotated various phases of the job. This freed the practice of design from the dead hand of caution, routine, and skepticism which makes new ideas shrivel before they can develop strength."[22]

For the next five years, Wurster was extremely active in educational reform, working to bring MIT's architectural department closer to the rest of the technically oriented school. He introduced a separate City and Regional Planning department and diversified the influences to which students at the schools were exposed. Under Wurster's guidance the school gained new prominence. Catherine taught part-time at Harvard and their daughter Sarah (named after Sarah Gregory) was born in 1945. Their house, near Christ Church, was always open to visitors, scholars, and students.

In 1946, Wurster brought Alvar Aalto from Finland to teach at MIT. If Wurster had an architectural idol, it was Aalto, whose Civic Center for Saynatsalo (built between 1948 and 1952) Wurster later deemed one of the most beautiful buildings in existence. While Aalto was at MIT, Wurster recommended him as architect for the Everett Moore Baker Residence Hall. The project caused a sensation not only at MIT but at Harvard as well. Walter Gropius and other faculty members celebrated the "change of attitude" that the Aalto commission signified.[23]

When Wurster became dean at MIT, he inherited a divergent faculty. With deft hiring and firing, he crafted a unique staff who held differing opinions about architectural design and city planning but was cohesive in their educational objectives. Wurster was a facilitator, not a mentor; he espoused no particular dogma, no singular idealist position. His administrative abilities are

reflected in the faculty Wurster brought to MIT: artist Gyorgy Kepes, critic Henry Russell Hitchcock, planner Kevin Lynch, and architects Eero Saarinen, Ralph Rapson, Carl Koch, Robert Woods Kennedy, Vernon DeMars, and Lloyd Rodwin.

Wurster believed that technology and the humanities must be linked and that the basis for architectural study is not the building itself, but its relationship to the people, the community, and to all other buildings—convictions that can be traced back to his tour of Europe in the 1920s. Wurster thought that architecture school should teach social research, economics, geography, and political science, and he felt that schools should set educational objectives that focus on regional characteristics. This would allow, even necessitate, that each school be different from every other.

Wurster and his faculty created a system where students had two or more critics assigned by the head of the architecture school, and this, according to Wurster, enabled the student to "taste the chaos which will be his when he meets the world."[24] These concepts changed the school dramatically from the cloistered confinement of the Beaux-Arts system to a curriculum that integrated architecture with the broad range of educational opportunities available at MIT. It thus became an intrinsic part of the university, not the isolated academy it had been before.

In addition to making MIT's architecture department both an interdisciplinary and an independent regional school, Wurster significantly influenced the campus building program. In a break from the traditional pattern of campus architectural development, Wurster wanted members of the faculty and other important architects to design new college buildings. The success of the dormitory designed by Aalto, coupled with Anderson and Beckwith's Alumni Swimming Pool of 1940, provided the impetus for proceeding with Wurster's suggestions.

Eastgate Faculty Housing, completed in 1949 and known simply as "100" (100 Memorial Drive), was designed by a collaborative Wurster shaped from the faculty that included Carl Koch, William Brown, Ralph Rapson, Vernon DeMars, and Robert Woods Kennedy. This initiated a building program at MIT that later included work by Eero Saarinen, I.M. Pei, Walter Netsch, Gordon Bunshaft, Eduardo

20. William Wurster at Berkeley, late 1950s

21. William Wurster and Catherine Bauer
Wurster, Istanbul, 1957

Catalano, Pietro Belluschi, Jose Sert, The Architect's Collaborative, Marvin Goody, and John Clancy.

In 1950, Wurster was asked by Chancellor Gordon Sproul (with the encouragement of Professor Jack Kent, Chairman of the Planning Department) to become the new dean of the architecture school at his alma mater, the University of California, Berkeley. Wurster always wanted to return to the West, and now he had the opportunity to rebuild the school that was so formative in his own career, a program whose reputation was still rooted in the Beaux-Arts curriculum. Under Wurster's guidance the architecture school became an institution of international stature that ultimately evolved into the College of Environmental Design at the University of California, Berkeley. [FIG. 20]

Wurster maintained that a healthy educational system "must be attacked with expressed doubts and enthusiasms and the changes which result should be ever-fluctuating."[25] He stressed that the school existed for its students and that the faculty must not be a refuge for the timid. He referred to the students' time in school and later in practice as the "architectural life" and considered a ten-year cycle of architectural education—five years in school followed by five more in an architectural practice—necessary to produce mature leadership in the profession. Wurster was eager to make the architect not a "special creature, but a creature of the world" with a well-rounded curriculum broadened, as at MIT, by study in fields other than architecture.[26] Wurster disagreed with the Bauhaus precept that architects should learn, as he described it, to become "plumbers" and

he ardently argued for the importance of having an inquiring mind. The force of Wurster's leadership was always directed toward defining a program that would ensure that students experienced in full the advantages of the rich life of the university.

Those first few years of exploration were not without pitfalls, and Wurster recalled that they held a curriculum-related symposium only to discover "that everybody was trying to make 'the whole man' every term and no one was teaching architecture."[27] It was during those tumultuous years that Wurster proved himself a "good administrator running fences for good teachers."[28] This may explain why Wurster was able to put together such extraordinary faculties. Wurster was not a revolutionary himself, but he did believe in what he called "controlled chaos, where there is no master school where one person sets the dominant note."[29] He often said, "I do not teach facts, but teach a process of arriving at facts."[30] He realized that students weren't necessarily comfortable with this approach because they would much rather have rote answers, but was convinced that years after graduation they would come to realize its value.

William Wurster did not consider himself a teacher, yet he was quite certain of what should be taught and sought people who could do it well. He introduced three courses under the direction of Charles Eames, Jesse Reichek, Philip Thiel, and James Prestini, two of which he described as aptitude tests that dealt with space and perception. The third course was an introduction to the professions and the broad disciplines of the university. Under the guidance of architect and historian Kenneth Cardwell, visiting lecturers discussed the importance of housing, aesthetics, urban sociology, business administration, economics, engineering, and interior design, as well as the professional disciplines of architecture, landscape architecture, and city and regional planning. Through these changes, Wurster introduced a counterbalance to the typical concentration on the creative aspects in the curriculum. These innovative programs at Berkeley dramatically shifted the emphasis of architectural education from merely drawing designs for buildings to understanding the design process itself. Wurster contended that no student should be forced to spend his or her life in the profession as a draftsperson because that was all that was taught in college.

In 1957, Wurster and his family embarked on an around-the-world trip during which he lectured extensively on architecture and education. [FIG. 21] These lectures gave him the opportunity to share his conviction that regional characteristics should be reflected in the man-made environment. When he returned, Wurster began realizing his long-held dream of uniting the three separate schools of Landscape Architecture, City and Regional Planning, and Architecture to form a single entity. Despite considerable internal resistance, Wurster's views prevailed. In 1959, when he was appointed the first Dean of the College of Environmental Design, Wurster said, "New problems evoke new answers and all institutions, including universities, must change to meet the challenge of the new."[31]

The term "environmental design" held no mystique for Wurster. He thought it was the appropriate designation since each of the professions—architecture, landscape architecture, city and regional planning, and visual design—plays a role in organizing and designing the physical environment for human needs. "It becomes necessary to be not only the master of one profession but also to have a real perception of the other disciplines in order to know how these may be integrated with one's own to produce a harmonious result."[32] The responsibilities in each profession demanded mutual contact and understanding and, being linked in so many ways, it was appropriate to bring them into a common college.

Wurster's home on Greenwood Common—the former house of Warren and Sarah Gregory in the Berkeley hills—became a meeting place for scholars and students, as had the Wurster home in Cambridge. Wurster continued the tradition begun by John Galen Howard of giving "tea" courses (in reference to the time of day and according to legend, in reference to the architect's T-square) for the graduating class, epitomized by spirited conversation and learning. Wurster also continued the school's practice of encouraging students to work under teachers who were meeting the contemporary requirements of professional practice.

As at MIT, Wurster was supervising architect of the campus planning committee, formulating a building policy that related the university's academic plan to the long-range development of its physical plan. At Berkeley, Wurster again promoted the idea that members of the faculty should design university buildings. In 1966, the new College of Environmental Design moved into a new structure designed by faculty members Joseph Esherick, Vernon DeMars, and Donald Olsen, the only project on which the three collaborated. The building, named Wurster Hall after both William and Catherine, was Wurster's pride and joy, and he reveled in the fact that it looked "like a ruin that no Regent would like...absolutely unfinished, rough, uncouth, and brilliantly strong."[33] Wurster Hall certainly marks a departure from campus architecture that imitated, in various ways, John Galen Howard's neoclassical buildings from the 1910s. Shortly before the building was completed, Wurster retired from his post as dean of the College of Environmental Design.

William Wurster became a father figure to many who taught in architecture schools around the United States. As the dean of two renowned schools, he espoused ideas that restructured architectural education and made major contributions to both the architectural profession and academic life for over four decades. His influence was considerable and is a lasting reminder of his belief that "the educator must always be aware that he operates not merely in the present, but, far more significantly, through his students, in the future."[34]

Wurster's practice continued to flourish after returning to California and becoming Dean

22. Ghiradelli Square Mixed-Use Development, San Francisco, 1963

23. Golden Gateway Development,
San Francisco, 1963

24. Center for Advanced Study of the Behavioral Sciences,
Stanford, California

25. Bank of America Headquarters, San Francisco, 1965

at Berkeley. Wurster's mature design intent is seen particularly in the houses where he had a demonstrable role and the sophisticated solutions he devised had recognizable links to his earliest work. The postwar building boom suited the well-established firm of Wurster, Bernardi & Emmons. The hundreds of projects from the partnership (located primarily in California) garnered international interest and influence and continued to be quite innovative. They included the first successful adaptive reuse project of Ghirardelli Square in San Francisco, the then-largest San Francisco office tower for the world's then-largest bank, Bank of America, as well as the Golden Gateway development which was the first of its kind in America—placing commercial on the street level and raising townhouses and residential towers on a podium above. Additionally, the firm created the first rural solution for academic conferencing. The design for the Center for Advanced Study of the Behavioral Sciences was integral to the development of the critical science of behavioral and social science pioneered at Stanford University.[35] [FIGS. 22–25]

In his mature work, Wurster's ideas were simplified and accentuated by their certainty of intent. He continued his commitment to regional architecture and to the art of building by pursuing the perfection of their appropriateness through his profound understanding of the physical, cultural, and historical meaning of the region and his recognition that architecture is primarily a response to human needs and aspirations.

Wurster's awareness of Northern and Central California's remarkable qualities is evidenced in his artlessly elegant yet eminently sensible residential designs, which always respected and never overshadowed their setting. His remarkable commercial and large residential projects also stemmed from his innate practicality and his ability to translate his ideals into simple, refined structures.

Wurster's accomplishments over the span of five decades were recognized twice by the American Institute of Architects (AIA), which in 1965 presented the Architecture Firm Award—its highest honor—to Wurster, Bernardi & Emmons.

Wurster also received the AIA's 1969 individual Gold Medal recognizing a "body of work of lasting influence on the theory and practice of architecture," a distinction he shared with his mentor William Adams Delano (1953) and friend Alvar Alto (1963).

In his capacity as dean of two distinguished architecture schools (MIT and Berkeley), Wurster's transformation of their educational philosophies exerted an immense and enduring impact on subsequent generations of architects and thus on the profession as we know it today. Wurster retired from his position as dean of Berkeley's College of Environmental Design in 1963. He died in 1973.

Wurster's steady insistence on making places that enfold the life of the place rather than impose an alien order was central to the development of the Bay Region variant of modern architecture in the United States. He pointed to a way of building that would be modest, fitted to the site and surroundings, and engaged with the landscape and regional ways of building. The relevance of this message is even clearer now.

Wurster's status as a "hidden" American treasure is primarily because of the simplicity of his designs, so subtle that their discernible influence on architecture has been muted. Wurster took a tradition begun by his visionary Bay Area predecessors (Bernard Maybeck, most obviously) and adapted it to his time, making it aesthetically "modern." He approached the design and building of a structure in a holistic way. Wurster melded together a consideration for landscaping, surrounding buildings, environment, and site with the innovative use of natural materials and local building techniques to achieve his main goal: enhancing contemporary lifestyles.

All good architects are inherently regional: their buildings respond in some measure to local climate, landscape, and site. While Wurster fully understood this basic premise, he reinterpreted the prevailing relationship among user, form, and landscape to reflect and allow for contemporary California lifestyles. It was within this regional vocabulary that Wurster's ingenuity changed the face of American and European architecture.

THE HOUSES OF WILLIAM WURSTER

1925

—

1931

THE EARLY YEARS

Starting out, William Wurster's new architecture
developed a regional response and garnered national fame,
reflecting the country's expansive spirit before it entered
the Great Depression.

Gillespie House

Oakland, California

This house was designed and built between 1925 and 1926. Wurster met Chester Gillespie, who was the Chief of the State Sanitation Board, while working on the San Leandro Filtration Plant. Gillespie wanted Wurster to create a small retreat in a pine forest in the Oakland Hills.

Unlike his earlier projects, this was the first that was not derived from European precedent. Before this, Wurster designed what his clients wanted, houses that reflected popular style as depicted in contemporary periodicals—that of revivalist architecture. Wurster's desire and ability to make homes that allowed for enjoyable living indoors and out was already in evidence in his earlier works (Elwood Wright House, Oakland, 1925), but this is the earliest example of the implementation of these ideas in a regional building language. The architecture became known as the "carpenter tradition"—using local materials and construction practices as the basis for architectural choices.

Wurster created an integrated response by designing and developing the house and gardens simultaneously (he said it took him only hours to design the house). The site plan shows the complete utilization of the grounds and gardens, and assimilates—even at this small scale—the lessons of designing landscape and building en masse, learned while Wurster worked for Delano and Aldrich, relating all spaces, inside and out, to each other and to a specific use or outlook.

Whimsical on the exterior with woodpecker brackets and green shutters, the interiors were more formal and reminiscent of the work of his mentors, John Galen Howard and Ernest Coxhead.

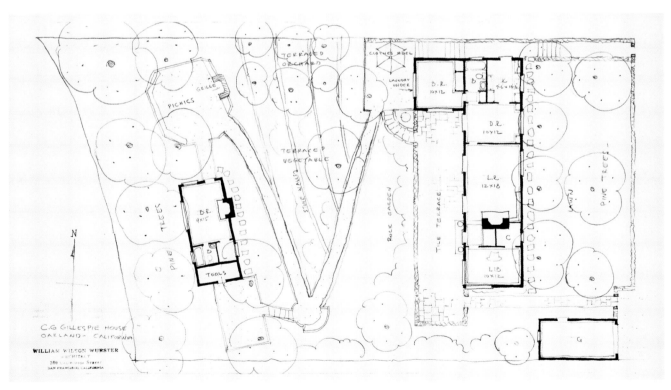

top left and right: Wurster's personal snapshots
bottom: Site and floor plan

37

[1927 and 1931]

Smith House

Berkeley, California

Concurrent with the Gillespie House, this French Regency townhouse was designed for two elderly sisters and built in 1927; it was completed with the addition of a design studio in a front wing in 1931. In the original design, on Wurster's insistence, the entry, living room, and dining room were painted a light green: "The entrance must have an appeal that draws a warmth to the person coming in."[1] The 1931 addition at the front of the property enclosed a small formal garden court and also provided an arched passageway that allowed entrance to the original entry at the living room wing. The courtyard plan allowed the living room to open to two private gardens and made this small house seem expansive despite its confined site.

Landscaping by the owner and William Wurster with "later advice by Lockwood deForest."[2]

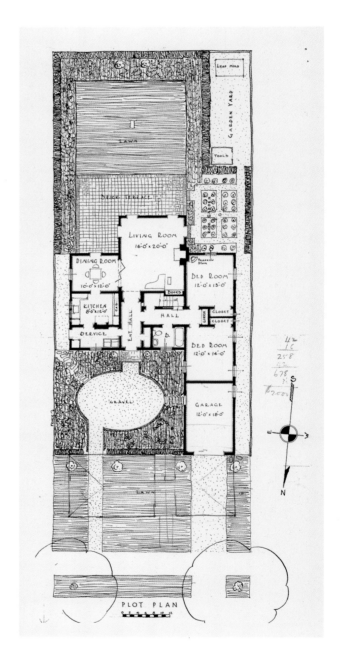

Wurster's early Smith plan

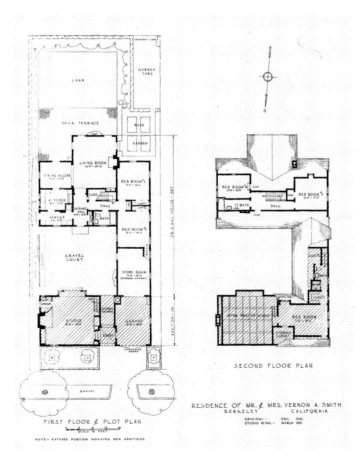

RESIDENCE OF MR. & MRS. VERNON A. SMITH
BERKELEY   CALIFORNIA
ORIGINAL -   DEC. 1926
STUDIO WING -   MARCH 1931

FIRST FLOOR & PLOT PLAN

SECOND FLOOR PLAN

NOTE:- HATCHED PORTION INDICATES NEW ADDITIONS

top: An early photograph shows the addition of the design
studio apartment and garage in front of the original living quarters.
bottom: Wurster's Smith plan, with addition

W. Gregory Farmhouse

Scott's Valley, California

Warren Gregory originally commissioned his good friend John Galen Howard, and his son Henry, to design a family farmhouse for summer retreats. The Gregorys had already been vacationing in another house on the property, which had been designed some years before by Howard on a site in a shady ravine. The family often picnicked on the site for the new house and had come to love the exposure and distant views to the Pacific Ocean. On the new site there was an existing water tower and rammed earth structure intended to function as a garage.[3] The Howard scheme for the new house from 1926—a cruciform plan to be built in rammed earth with ornate Italianate features—was abandoned by Sarah Gregory after her husband's unexpected death in 1927. Later that year, she asked Wurster to redesign the project. Legend has it that she had previously toured Wurster's completed projects and felt that the carpenter-tradition of the Gillespie house in the Oakland Hills embodied the aesthetics that she found most fitting as the basis for the design of the farmhouse summer retreat.

In October 1927, Wurster made a sketch on his first visit to the site with Sarah Gregory and her good friend, Elizabeth Ellis, and the house was built almost without alteration to the original design. The working drawings were finished six days after the initial sketch. The construction began in December, and the house was completed the following spring. It was a designed for a temperate setting that gracefully blurred the distinction between indoor and outdoor living. The farmhouse as a collection of linked forms copied no traditional forms; rather, it embodied the

region's essential spirit as conceived by a creative genius. Wurster took vernacular references and made architecture. Wurster later wrote that the following fundamentals governed the project (somewhat paraphrased): First, appropriateness of the building to the site, the house was to be long and low and built around an early California "yard," and was paved with the endgrain stumps of redwoods cut in the area. Second, simple living; there is no dining room, meals are eaten on a porch. For privacy and to avoid halls, rooms are entered from the exterior. Third, modest cost; fundamental principles that need to be maintained were a good roof, foundation, and draft-free walls. Otherwise, no plaster, just whitewashed board walls. Fourth, no garden upkeep; entrance yard is an arid space, with terraces for living and games. The goal was to leave the place closed up for long intervals without worry.[4]

Elements that were critical for the success of this project were the forecourt facade, relatively closed to the west, while circulation between rooms occurred along an outside covered passageway along this edge. The yard, with its redwood stump paving and covered walkway, provided shelter from the midday sun. Additionally, the Large Room had a taller form than the rest and an interior ceiling over 9 feet high. Overall, the focus of the rooms was away from the protected court and toward the south patio with views southeast toward the ocean and due east for morning light. All of these rooms had a finished floor close to the grade so that the transition from inside to outside seems to be without a threshold. Wurster later reflected: "The place is intended as a contrast to

opposite: **View through the living room, toward the gallery and court**

the complications of city and professional life and each decision was influenced by a desire for simplicity." Until the early 1940s—thirteen years after completion—the house had no electricity.[5]

This country house was a turning point in Wurster's career. Although it did not gain recognition until 1931 when it won *House Beautiful*'s Small Home Award, it enabled Wurster to pursue his ideas about simple and practical building. His design ideas were rooted in his rural Californian upbringing, generated first from his admiration of the Craftsman buildings and later expounded in the houses he designed in the hills of Oakland and Berkeley. The Gregory farmhouse eloquently responded to the special climate of the rolling coastal hills with native oaks and manzanita, and it recalled California ranch houses. The house's studied naturalness reflects Wurster's innate understanding, as a native son of California, of the underlying intent of traditional building forms and the simplicity of local building practices.

Sally Woodbridge wrote of the house, "It took the body of Modern Architecture and gave it a regional soul."[6]

As with most of his work in this and later periods, Wurster's design for the Gregory farmhouse was based on an interpretation of the modern family—a family without servants and a family wanting to live in closer relationship to the outdoors. He was not concerned with the notion of a "modern" architecture since his work typically consisted of simplified versions of prevailing accepted styles. Wurster's work, although far from other "modern" architectural examples at the time, stood in sharp contrast to popular published work from the East and West coasts that valued the literal revival of traditional styles. In a reflection nearly ten years after the farmhouse's completion, Wurster wrote to Sarah Gregory, "The sense of the deep inner rightness about the Farm tells of the realization in site, structure and atmosphere, of the richness and the reality of the life around which it was conceived."[7]

left: View of the entry. Bedrooms are at the front and the living room, with a taller
roof line and ceiling, is tucked into the corner of the L-shaped plan.
right: View across the courtyard paved with redwood stumps, toward the tower

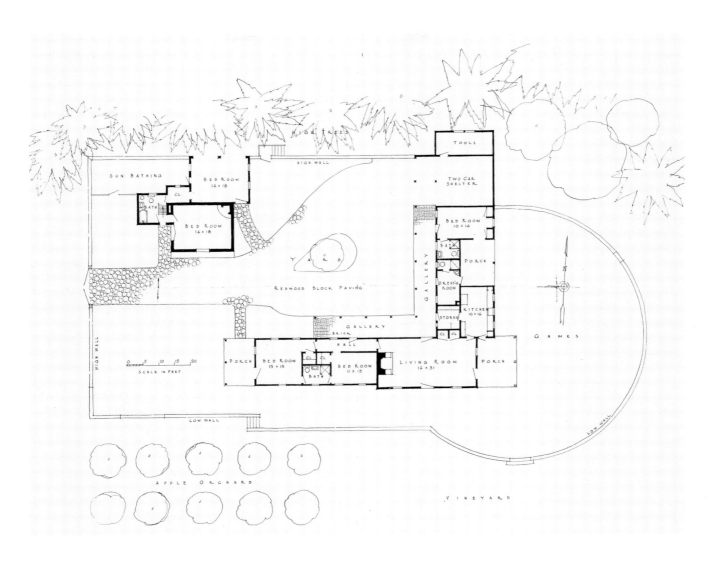

SUN BATHING

BED ROOM
14 x 18

CL

BATH

HIGH WALL

HIGH TREES

BED ROOM
14 x 18

YARD

REDWOOD BLOCK PAVING

TOOLS

TWO CAR
SHELTER

BED ROOM
10 x 16

BATH

DRESS'G
ROOM

KITCHEN
10 x 16

STORES

PORCH

GALLERY

GAMES

0   5   10   15   20
SCALE IN FEET

HIGH WALL

PORCH

BED ROOM
15 x 15

CL CL

BATH

GALLERY

BRICK

HALL

BED ROOM
11 x 15

CL CL

LIVING ROOM
16 x 31

PORCH

LOW WALL

LOW WALL

APPLE ORCHARD

VINEYARD

top: The farmhouse floor and site plan clearly defined the uses of indoor and outdoor spaces.
bottom: The living room, as it was furnished soon after completion.
The floor is made of 12-inch boards and the ceilings are over 10 feet high.

The water tower and attached rammed-earth bedroom

left: The "big room" today
right: View from the western bedroom to the covered porch

Kellam House

Santa Barbara, California

This house built in Santa Barbara, California, for the parents of landscape architect Lockwood deForest's wife, Elizabeth Kellam, was Wurster's first residential adaptation of what he termed the Monterey style, and the furthest south that Wurster designed homes. Undoubtedly inspired by his knowledge of old California houses in Monterey, Wurster chose to use these simpler influences rather than the more flamboyant Spanish Colonial interpretations prevalent in the area, such as George Washington Smith's Hope Ranch. Wurster's instinct for the potential of the site produced a handsome ensemble that was orderly, unforced, and restrained in its fenestration and details.

The house was sited next door to a house that deForest had designed for himself. The compound was established on three acres nestled behind the Santa Barbara Mission. Both houses and their gardens faced northeast toward the dramatic views of Cathedral Peak and the Santa Barbara mountain range. The traditional L-shaped plan was splayed so that, while shaping the gardens, all rooms could enjoy distant views without looking toward the bulk of the building. The high front porch faced south and furnished welcome shade to the entry and the front court while also providing outdoor access to the second-floor bedrooms and a view to the Pacific Ocean and the vibrant sunsets.

Wurster and deForest attended Berkeley for their last year of schooling in 1919 and along with Thomas Church, became acquainted there. Wurster was chosen for the commission in part because of this, and in large part because the Kellams received a glowing endorsement from their East Coast acquaintance (and Wurster's former employer), William Delano.

This was the first of at least ten projects that Wurster and deForest undertook together. Throughout the years Wurster often referenced his friendships and professional partnerships with the deForests and the Churchs.

opposite, top and bottom: The house seen from the front courtyard.
The roof over the front porch was recently added.

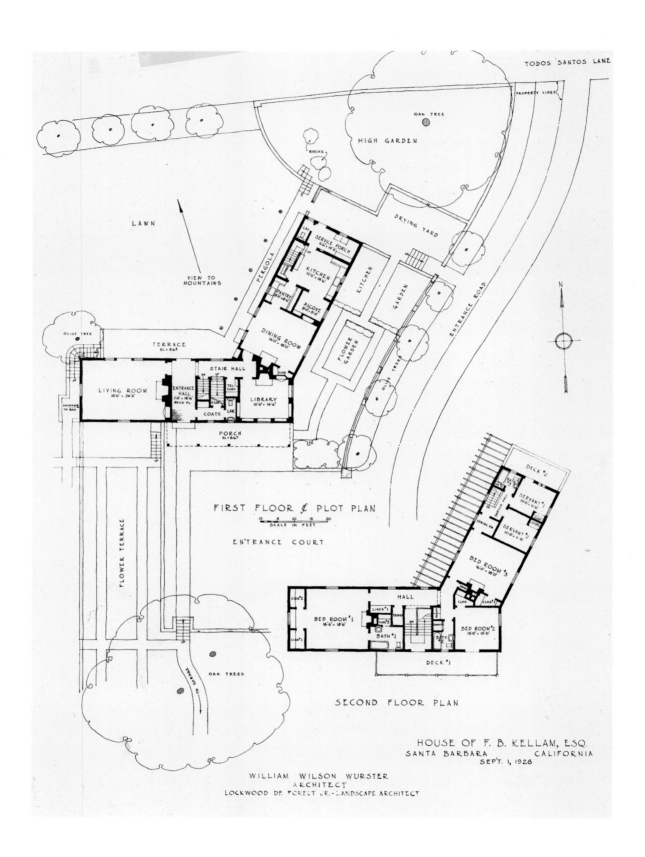

FIRST FLOOR & PLOT PLAN

SECOND FLOOR PLAN

HOUSE OF F. B. KELLAM, ESQ.
SANTA BARBARA   CALIFORNIA
SEP'T. 1, 1928

WILLIAM WILSON WURSTER
ARCHITECT
LOCKWOOD DE FOREST JR.—LANDSCAPE ARCHITECT

Site and floor plan

top: Entry elevation, from Lockwood DeForest Jr.'s adjacent driveway
left: The front door, from the entrance court
right: Elizabeth Kellam DeForest walking in the new garden

Hagar House

Berkeley, California

Perched on a steep hillside in the Berkeley hills with a commanding view to the south and the west of San Francisco Bay, is the Hagar House, a Mediterranean villa built in 1928. The Hagars wanted a house that "could capture the romantic spirit of California" and said that Wurster's first sketch was "perfect almost to the finest detail."[8] The stark simplicity of the entrance court facade belies the gracious and comfortable scale of the interior spaces. The well-proportioned living room with its vaulted, crisply detailed mahogany ceiling and white plaster walls displays Wurster's sense of simple elegance. The immaculate detailing is characteristic of his tendency to pare away all the unessential elements and "let things be

expressed as they are."[9] Designed concurrently with the Gregory's farmhouse in Scott's Valley, this was to be a city house; a full-time residence, although designed with minimal embellishments, it still is clearly referential to Mediterranean architecture in its massing details and material choices.

Most of the rooms have direct access to the outdoors and natural light from at least two sides. Despite the often-dark interior of traditional Mediterranean architecture, Wurster didn't compromise the pleasurable qualities of the rooms to suit a formal arrangement for the architecture. Gardens credited to Lockwood deForest have outdoor garden rooms that were an extension of the interior.[10]

above, left and right: The Hagar House in 1928
opposite: Side view, present day

opposite: Little has changed on the main floor of the house,
but one exception is the addition of this glass canopy over the front door.
left: Entry court with stair window
right: A modest and effective south-facing stair window adjacent to the front door
provides a well of natural light to the interior staircase.

left and right: The living room in Wurster's
snapshot from the 1920s, and the room today
opposite: Living room view

Hollins House

Pasatiempo, Santa Cruz, California

Marion Hollins, the famed golfer and developer, established the golfing community of Pasatiempo and she hired Wurster to build "all the buildings" for the development (see pages 23–24).[11] For her own house, Marion Hollins chose a site on a steep hillside wooded with oaks. Overlooking a ravine, it had distant views to the Pacific Ocean. Wurster was instructed to design a house without removing any trees. Hollins, having grown up in a wealthy New York family who summered on Long Island, wanted a country retreat that suited her personal needs for comfort. The Hollins house is the most formal in scale and detailing of the Wurster houses at Pasatiempo.

This house needed to reflect Hollins's sensibilities honed as a child of the Gatsby era. It was to be a simplified version of the comfortable life enjoyed on Long Island's summer estates that still represented the Pasatiempo motto of being a place set apart "to preserve the Spanish tradition of leisure to enjoy life."[12] Its exterior architectural detailing was similar to the nearby W. Gregory house in Scotts Valley, but its design was much more formal. The Gregory house was simpler in both its intent and plan. Hollins's house, Wurster's first effort on a hillside with this architectural language, was much more complicated. It shifted the plan and levels to adjust to the curving hillside contours allowing all rooms to have a unique and direct relationship to the landscape and distant views, and to maximize the appreciation of the sun and shade of the site.

Entered from the north it was critical to Hollins that the garden be completely screened from the entry and service sides of the house.

Approached by walking down through a grove of oak trees, the large front door was the only welcoming spot: "It always seems more welcoming to have a generous door particularly when going down the hill against it."

A variation on typical early California ranch architecture, the building appeared as a connected grouping of traditional structures: farm outbuildings of lightweight wood-stud construction were joined to the more substantial thick-walled main house. The articulation of materials and details set up a language of contrasts: horizontal board-and-batt wood siding and smooth stucco, deep-set and shallow windows and doors, and a combination of gable and shed roofs with both types shifting from generous to minimal eaves depending upon the purpose and exposure. The interior rooms of the main spaces were finished in painted, smooth, and wide horizontal redwood boards with extensive moldings. The main interior spaces varied between 11- and 12-feet tall—"it gives you and airiness and freedom not possessed by a low ceiling bearing down upon your head."[13] The plan for the inside of the house reflected the variety of the exterior's features. Hollins's living room was connected via a narrow balcony on the exterior and a large, simply constructed exterior wooden spiral stair to an outdoor dining room called the "kitchen cave" with a brick-on-grade floor that extended beyond the house as a terrace and became integrated with the gardens by Thomas Church. "There is great joy gained always by contrast and I have made the cave the low and intimate thing."[14] This was the first of Wurster's many inside-outside dining spaces.

top: The main entry, originally approached by descending through a grove of old oak trees
bottom: The original colored sketch of the garden side. The living room connection can be seen,
as well as the grove of mature oaks that surrounded the house.

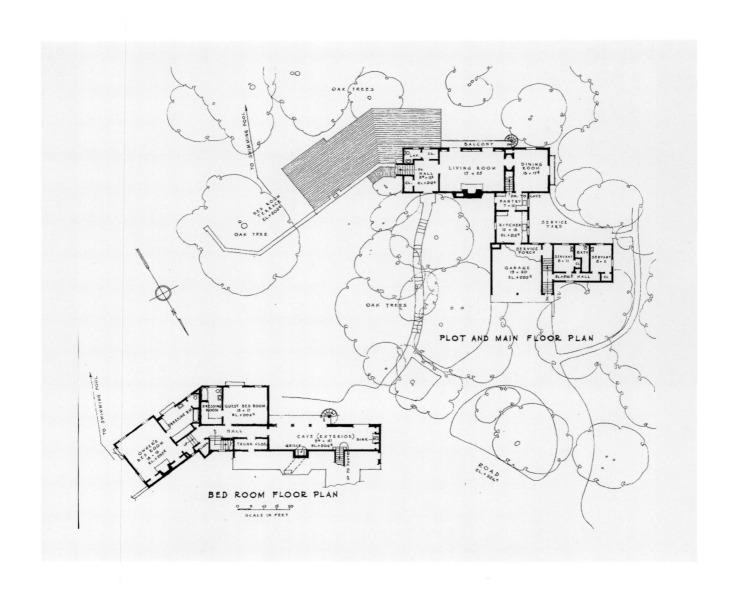

PLOT AND MAIN FLOOR PLAN

BED ROOM FLOOR PLAN

SCALE IN FEET

The site and floor plan show how the house weaves though an existing
oak grove while screening the garden from the road.

top: View from ravine toward the kitchen cave
bottom: The kitchen cave

The bedroom wing and screen wall,
seen from the southeast side of the bedroom terrace

above: The living room looks much as it did when first designed.
overleaf: The terrace recently replaced a much smaller and simpler wood balcony,
connecting the living room directly to the garden and kitchen cave.

General Manager's House (Kaplansky-Howes)

Pasatiempo, Santa Cruz, California

Marion Hollins had a house built for the general manager of Pasatiempo.[15] The house also served as a sales office and as a model home for potential property buyers and architectural clients.

When designing Marion Hollins's house Wurster had a client with tastes formed by a New Yorker's aesthetics for ornament—the General Manager's house was designed to reflect the motto of Pasatiempo, "preserving the Spanish Tradition."[16] Wurster interpreted this to mean a house with a simpler palette of details, one that was probably closer to his own ideals.

As at Hollins's home, Wurster loosely linked simple rural forms. Its central volume had 12-foot ceilings and thickened wood-frame walls, which served as the entry, living room, and dining room. "As this country is influenced by the presence of California adobe structures the walls of certain portions are furred to give a thickness as adobe walls."[17] Similar to adobe architecture the openings are deep set with flared sides to draw in and capture light. These openings are few but generously scaled and the windows double as light-flooded seating areas. The only doorway to the courtyard from the living room is 5 feet by 8 feet.

In order to emphasize the "adobe" character, the interior and exterior thickened walls were finished in rough exterior-grade stucco. Unusual in these rooms, but a precedent-setter for Wurster, was the use of wide, painted redwood boards to finish all of the ceilings and the internal walls.[18] There's an early example in this house of how Wurster would clad minor interior doors (closets and bathrooms) with exterior siding to match adjacent walls. Without trim, these doors disappeared from view and helped focus attention on the doors that really counted.[19] The floors throughout are bricks on grade, with a finish and pattern that extends outside to the courtyard. "The floors are of waxed brick as it was thought desirable to allow for muddy boots from golf."[20]

The central, more massive volume was extended by two wood-sided, traditionally constructed wings. One wing had a gallery open to the courtyard, which contained the service areas and connected a roadside entrance for potential

above: The house, seen from the road
opposite, top: The courtyard view with its fountain and sitting wall
opposite, bottom: The main entry

customers and the adobe-style sales office and guest bedroom to the central courtyard. The second wing had a parallel gallery, which was glazed, and connected bedrooms to the courtyard and the main body of the house. Glazing a passageway and using external finishes in internal spaces, was seen in this project for the first time and became a hallmark of Wurster's work.

The entire architectural assembly of this house was organized around a south-facing lawn and brick court raised above the adjacent landscape. Wurster's design intended that the courtyard be the primary method of circulating through the house "making it necessary to go through the living room to [reach] the bedrooms in bad weather."[21] The court was raised about 4 feet above the public road and had a low sitting wall to enclose it, which kept the courtyard private from the road and the golf course. The views south to the Monterey Bay and peninsula were maintained from within the court. A central two-sided fountain served as a symbol of community and as a welcoming amenity for watering the club members' horses, a dominant part of the Pasatiempo lifestyle.

Over all, the consistent use of shake roofing and white tones over the varied textures of the stucco and wood-sided house and garden walls married the various forms into a unified whole.

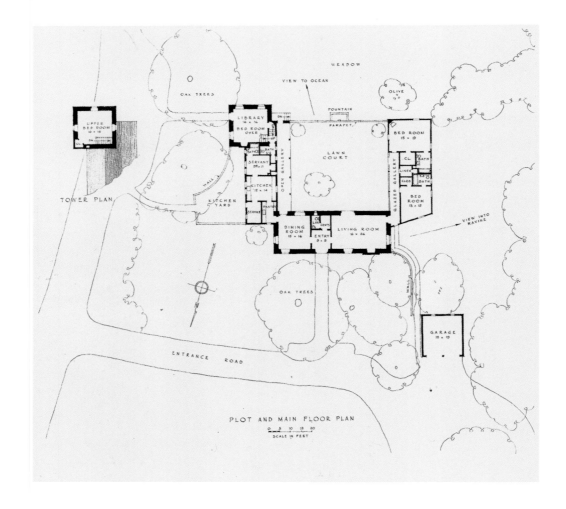

The floor and site plan incidates how the design provides access to the critical views and environmental opportunities.

above: Two views of the main rooms of the house.
The lower shows the diagonal placement of the bedroom wall,
allowing for the living room's view to the distant ravine.

top: The courtyard and the wisteria-clad glazed bedroom gallery
bottom: The living room, looking toward the glazed bedroom gallery and courtyard
opposite: Detail of the entry

Sloss House

Woodside, California

On a 75-acre estate in Woodside, established as an extended family summer retreat for a prominent San Francisco family, this house for one of the daughters is reminiscent of an early California ranch house. Built in 1930, twenty years after Greene and Greene built "the big house" on the property, this summerhouse is located on the site of the estate's original tennis court. Similar in spirit to the Sherwood Ranch located near Salinas in Monterey County, it is a rambling redwood shake house built as an L around a large level courtyard.[22] The glazed gallery entry is finished as an exterior space. As with many of his projects, Wurster has obscured most of the doors in this room and emphasized the two primary doorways with wide, heavy, somewhat ornamental detailing.

The flooring in the gallery is an extension, with little threshold, of the brick courtyard. The gallery effectively connects the sleeping and the living spaces, maintaining complete privacy from each other. Remodeled soon after by Wurster, the original design had most of the bedrooms as screened porches and a tower for the children's sleeping quarters.[23] The use of screened spaces continues into a gracious dining room, which is detailed in redwood paneling and molding—a similar tone as his other sheltered outdoor spaces, but with the detailing reflecting a more formal tradition. Hexagonal in shape, the corner windows/doors of the dining room open up completely to screened panels, which allows natural breezes to cool the room. Both Lockwood deForest and Thomas Church were involved in the gardens of this house.

top: The garden of the Green Gables House by Greene and Greene, the original estate house
opposite, top: The Sloss House entry gallery
opposite, bottom: The porte cochere, outside the children's tower

top: The courtyard entry frames the children's sleeping porch in the tower.
bottom: View showing the relationship of the gallery, tower, and porte cochere, to the courtyard.

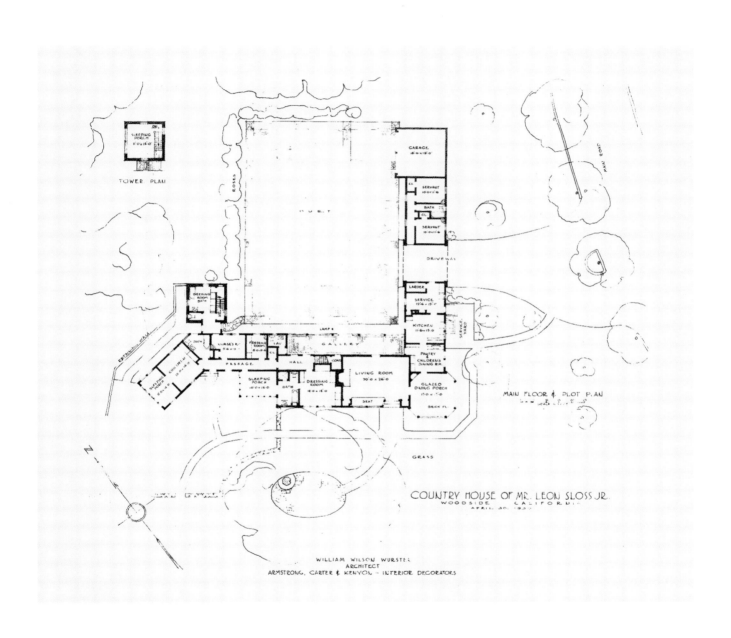

above: Site and floor plan showing how the house was designed with
numerous screened sleeping porches and points of entry.
overleaf, left: Inside the porte cochere, an example of blind doors
overleaf, right: View from the courtyard back toward the road

above: Entrance doors at the gallery
opposite and overleaf: Detail of glazing systems, allowing a variety of ways to ventilate.
The exposed roof framing, exterior siding, minimal window sill,
and waxed brick flooring create a minimal boundary between inside and out.

left, right, opposite: The octagonal dining porch was designed with
screened openings to provide natural ventilation.

Mackenzie House

Pasatiempo, Santa Cruz, California

Alastair Mackenzie, a British surgeon and golf course designer, had already laid out the golf course at Augusta National in Georgia when he came to California to help Marion Hollins with the new course at Cypress Point in Monterey for the Del Monte Corporation. In exchange for his participation at Pasatiempo, Mackenzie was given this parcel and his home was designed and built for him.[24]

This small, one-bedroom house, which was shielded from the street by a grove of oak trees, used some of the same ideas seen in the other Pasatiempo houses. Tall walls extending from the small house screened the living spaces and private garden—initially it is difficult to distinguish wall from house. In fact, early additions to the house, first by Wurster and then by others, incorporated the walls seamlessly into new interior spaces.

From the golf course side, the modest and elegant gabled structure and its Thomas Church gardens were framed by the extended walls and grove of oaks behind it. Like the General Manager's house, which has its largest and most welcoming entry toward the courtyard, Mackenzie's screened veranda opens the house generously to the fairway. Appropriately, the veranda served as Mackenzie's front door—welcoming golfers during their round.[25]

above: Sketch of the house, ca. 1930
opposite, top: Site and floor plan showing how the long garden wall ties all of the
parts of the house together, providing a screen between the golf course and the road.
opposite, bottom: The screen porch

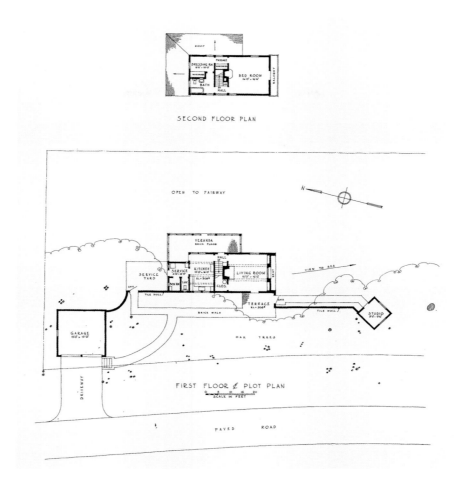

SECOND FLOOR PLAN

FIRST FLOOR & PLOT PLAN

SCALE IN FEET

Berry/Lombardi House

Pasatiempo, Santa Cruz, California

This long and narrow house for Berry and his niece and nephew is a modest solution for its country setting. Sited below the road because of the contours of the site, one sees over it to the ravine and oak trees beyond. As were many of Wurster's houses at Pasatiempo, this house was designed for summer and weekend use. The site is steeply sloped with views (and the hot summer sun) to the southeast. Wurster designed the south-facing, tree-shaded porch to be off the entry level; because of the slope it is raised a full story above the grade below. Built parallel to the slope, this whitewashed-board residence has a simple plan of lined-up rooms accessible from the spacious porch, used as the primary space for circulation to adjacent rooms, and holds both a sleeping and sunbathing area. By placing the kitchen and indoor-outdoor dining room on the lower level, a level below the entry and living room, Wurster linked the house and its daily activities to gardens designed by Thomas Church. This house won numerous national awards including the coveted *House Beautiful* first prize, published in February 1937.

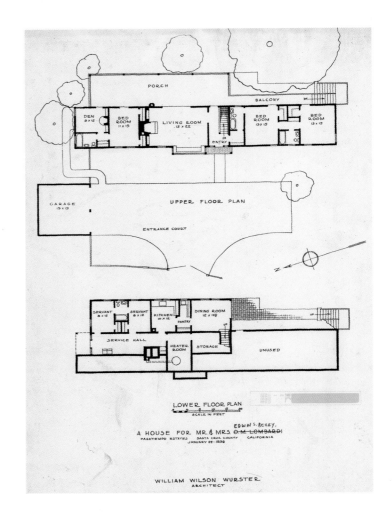

above: Site and floor plan
opposite: View of the first-floor dining room. Shade is
provided by the surrounding oak grove.

Church House

Pasatiempo, Santa Cruz, California

Wurster designed this house in what he termed his "modified modern style." Located on a sloped site overlooking a ravine, the house served to retain and create a flat open grass court toward the east "entry terrace" and across for the golf course.[26] To the west, the "living terrace" at a lower level overlooked the azalea- and oak-filled ravine.[27] The drafting room, which doubled as Church's office for seeing new Pasatiempo clients, was devised for maximum natural light. With a simple shed roof, the drafting studio had one large shed roof running the length of the room with 12-foot-tall, north-facing box-bay windows. It was this space that determined the composition of the house plan and its relationship to the site. All of the walls on the interior and exterior were finished with wide whitewashed redwood boards laid horizontally. Wurster believed the design was characterized by "simplicity, purity of design, poverty of embellishment, and turning away from imitation. The honesty of construction marks this as living art."[28]

above: Design proposal
opposite, top: The north-facing dormers of the former work studio
opposite, bottom: Church's drafting room

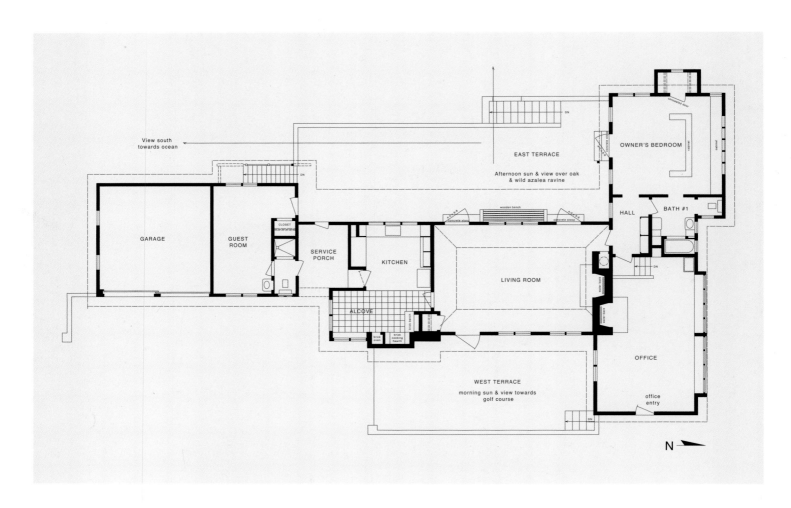

above: Floor plan
bottom: The studio and client entrance on the right
opposite: Detail of shed dormers in the former studio

Voss House

Big Sur, California

Built along Big Sur's hillside Santa Lucia coast, the house was designed to frame spectacular panoramas. Wurster declared Voss "an ideal client with an ideal site."[29] The Voss family wanted a house that provided respite from the summer heat of their hometown, Salinas, located just over the coastal mountain range in California's Central Valley. They were inspired by the Gregory farmhouse but wanted a house not so spread out.

Entered from the north, there was a desire for no openings other than the front door so as to maximize the light and views to the south and away from the prevailing weather from the northwest. Like some other Wurster houses, the living room doubled as a guest bedroom and couches were chosen to be large enough to sleep on comfortably; therefore, a dressing room on the main level was a necessity. The living room had large pocket French doors that were half the length of the room and which "on a good day will make the room seem to be part of the whole coast line."[30] The only bedroom was designed to open up to a porch big enough for sleeping. Continuing the theme of opening up the house entirely to the landscape, the kitchen and dining area were located on the lower floor and was a further developed version of the "kitchen cave." The floor was waxed brick and extended without a threshold to a terrace in a desire to "have a portion of the ground intimate with the house for out-of-door living."[31] Large bi-fold doors opened up much of the lower floor dining area to the view and southern sun.

The house is reminiscent of the vernacular barn construction typical along California's coast. With its large porch in the Monterey tradition on the upper level designed to "give protection in storms—[give] a fine shadow for appearance and cut down on any possible 'high' look."[32] Wurster sided the house with vertical redwood boards on the upper level, and horizontal boards on the lower "to provide variety."[33] In explaining the appeal of the Voss house, Wurster later recommended to an enquiring architect from the northeast region of the United States: "Be sure and have the board with a rough or resawn [sic] surface as such seems to become the simple life of a summer place."[34]

With the widespread publication of this house, Wurster's reputation was not only firmly established in the United States, but also his architectural aesthetics were of interest to the new form of Modernism being explored in Germany.

top: The kitchen cave
left: Floor and site plan
right: Cliffside view from the Pacific

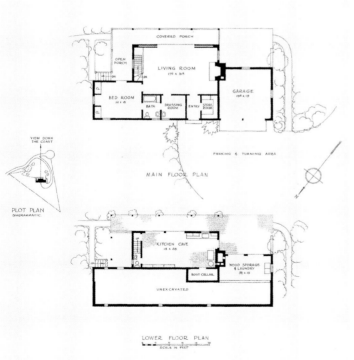

COVERED PORCH

OPEN
PORCH

LIVING ROOM
17'6 x 31'5

GARAGE
19'6 x 19'

BED ROOM
14 x 15

BATH

DRESSING
ROOM

ENTRY

STORE
ROOM

VIEW DOWN
THE COAST

PARKING & TURNING AREA

MAIN FLOOR PLAN

PLOT PLAN
DIAGRAMMATIC.

KITCHEN CAVE
13 x 28

WOOD STORAGE
& LAUNDRY
28 x 13

ROOT CELLAR

UNEXCAVATED

LOWER FLOOR PLAN

SCALE IN FEET

RESIDENCE OF MR. & MRS. C.L.VOSS
COAST LANDS   MONTEREY COUNTY   CALIFORNIA
NOVEMBER 4, 1931.

1933

1938

MIDDLE PHASE

William Wurster's national reputation was established
and his work began to be disseminated in European journals.
His architecture continued to reflect his earlier ideals
but his use of site, materials, and form became more inventive.

Benner House

Berkeley, California

This is a stucco house tucked into a small canyon in Berkeley. Although it presents itself as modern with its curved upper balcony, the design uses similar strategies as Wurster's houses that were intended primarily for casual use. As he wrote to the Benners in 1932: "I am all for the fresh views and the careful examination of this so-called modern, even though I am not for it lock, stock and barrel. It is very worth careful thought for it opens new vistas and enlivens the old."[1]

A multipurpose, enclosed ground-floor sun porch opens to a landscape by Thomas Church; it faces south, which made it an ideal playroom or retreat in winter or summer for Benner's large and active family. Like the Hollins and the Voss houses' kitchen caves, the sun porch is an extension of the garden landscape, and because of its central location, it also functioned as an indoor-outdoor living room. A south-facing balcony above the brick-floored sun porch connected the primary living spaces on the second floor to a sleeping porch and deck, both of which faced west to the Golden Gate.

In this particular plan for a city house used year-round, Wurster employed his strategy of designing for a more relaxed style of living that he also used for vacation houses. By placing the entry at the knuckle of a L-shaped plan, the living room was freed up to enjoy the majestic Bay views while maintaining an intimate relationship to the garden. This also provided opportunity to give the room the typical Wurster quality of well-balanced natural light. Like many of his weekend houses, every public room and all of the bedrooms (except the nurse's) have direct access to the gardens and communal balconies. It is a year-round house that idealizes the notion of indoor and outdoor living. Wurster wrote to Delano of this project, "We are in the throes of designing a house which shall take a fresh viewpoint—call it modern if you will but it is not to be reactionary modern—in a word, everything is done because of a positive wish never to be different—and I hope it will give a pleasant, enlightened look—but not bizarre."[2] Several years later, Wurster designed a pool and recreation structure for the Benners in nearby Orinda (1937).

top: The children's balcony above the sun porch's folding doors
bottom: Bird's-eye sketch

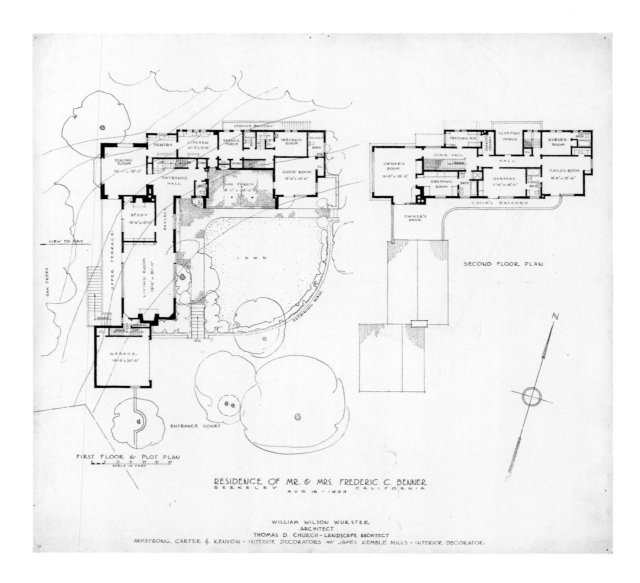

RESIDENCE OF MR. & MRS. FREDERIC C. BENNER
BERKELEY AUG. 16-1933 CALIFORNIA

WILLIAM WILSON WURSTER
ARCHITECT
THOMAS D. CHURCH - LANDSCAPE ARCHITECT
ARMSTRONG, CARTER & KENYON - INTERIOR DECORATORS W. JAMES KEMBLE MILLS - INTERIOR DECORATOR.

top: The site and floor plan show how the rooms are arranged to have
optimal solar and view exposure in an otherwise shady setting.
bottom: View from across the garden, toward the sun porch and children's balcony

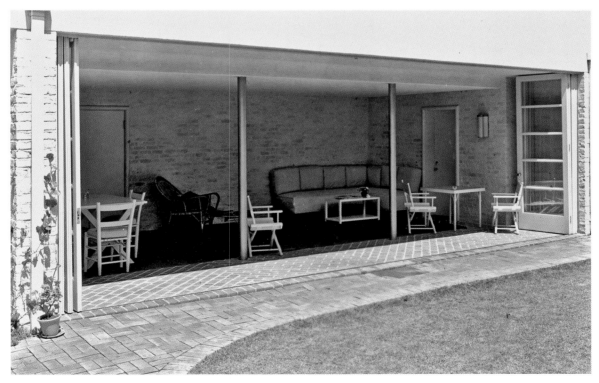

top: View west toward the living room
bottom: The owner's porch

Butler House

Pasatiempo, Santa Cruz, California

Sited with views east toward Monterey Bay, this house was designed as four evenly spaced pavilions, each approximately 20 square feet. The pavilions formed the corners of a large court-yard that surrounded an old live oak tree and were linked together by covered passageways and a service wing. In reflection, he remarked that the success of this project, in its useability and modesty, was achieved when he chose to spread out the spaces as far from each other as feasible.[3] The dominant room was an open gallery space that was called the "living porch"; it had a wood ceiling painted "sky blue" facing east toward the distant views.[4] The living porch allowed for

informal living and dining while enjoying a beautiful shaded outlook. With a large fireplace, this living porch could be enjoyed even in cool weather. The use of the gallery as an important living space became another of Wurster's trade-mark spaces. This was the first clear example, however, of Wurster formalizing a porch or breeze-way into a easily habitable room with entry doors and a fireplace. The tree-centered drive court functioned as a central gathering space as well, so there was little sense of a formal entrance; inhabitants interacted seamlessly with the natural surroundings.

above: The so-called "living porch"
opposite, top: View from the covered passage through the porch
opposite, bottom: Floor and site plan

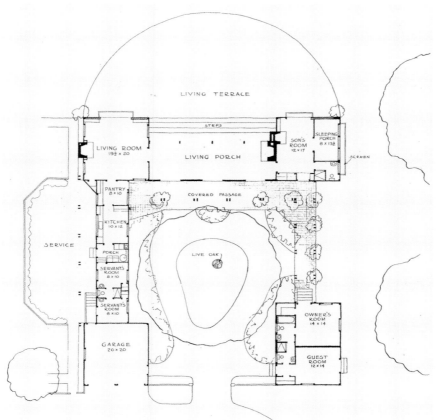

LIVING TERRACE

STEPS

LIVING ROOM
19½ × 20

LIVING PORCH

SON'S ROOM
12 × 17

SLEEPING PORCH
8 × 13½

SCREEN

PANTRY
8 × 10

COVERED PASSAGE

KITCHEN
10 × 12

SERVICE

PORCH

LIVE OAK

SERVANTS ROOM
8 × 10

SERVANTS ROOM
8 × 10

OWNER'S ROOM
14 × 14

GARAGE
20 × 20

GUEST ROOM
12 × 14

[1935]

Kenyon Cottage Apartments

San Francisco, California

The gray and white clapboard apartments are designed as a group of interlocking cottages that cascade down the steep hillside. Located on Russian Hill in San Francisco, each apartment is staggered so that minimal living space overlaps. Its plan is reminiscent of the ingenuity of Greek village architecture, the units are integrally connected to each other and accessed by a simple common stair system that allows each unit to have a private front courtyard and one tree at a minimum. Kenyon rented out the three smaller units (two studio apartments and a two-bedroom unit) and lived in the fourth.[5] Her rear-most unit (Cottage One) is two stories and had three bedrooms (including a servant's quarters). It is a complicated site and it must have been challenging to find a graceful solution that allowed for a distinct character for each unit while still maintaining a sense of a unified whole to the street. Additionally, it is quite remarkable that as many as three private outdoor spaces exist for each of the units. Designed to maximize the tremendous views toward the San Francisco Bay as well as to respond to the complex climate of marine weather patterns, Wurster's design allows for protection as well as exposure in all of the spaces, whether indoor or out. This building is one of Wurster's seminal urban buildings in a city where gardens, privacy, and views are highly valued.

above: The cottages from the street. The Hamill House balcony can be seen in the upper left.
opposite: View from the entry court into the living room of Cottage One

top: View of entry to Cottage Four
bottom: The living room of Cottage Three

above: Views of private deck off of the living room and dining room of Cottage One
overleaf: Originally a screened sun porch, it is now a sitting room adjacent to the master bedroom.

Miller House

Carmel, California

This house, designed for a young woman just after she had completed her studies at the University of California, Berkeley, is sited on hillside overlooking the Pacific Ocean coast.[6] The house was designed for Diantha Miller to use as a weekend house for herself and friends while enjoying the beaches a few minutes drive away. It is a small turquoise-colored house that, by hugging the slope and looking outward toward the ocean views beyond, embraced the grandeur of the seaside. "The long sweep of [the] hills made anything but a simple roof line seem trifling."[7] Wurster's choice of color (which is seen repeated in some of his other houses that relate to the Pacific Ocean) was based on it being "the same color as the sky and the sea."[8]

As with many of his smaller houses, this one seems larger than it is. In this case, Wurster does it by borrowing the expansive views in all directions—to the west to scenic Point Lobos on the Pacific Ocean and the old adobe Carmel Mission, south toward a large open-space preserve with a dramatic ridgeline, and east up the Carmel Valley. To the north, the house is essentially closed except for an 8-foot-tall "dutch" entry door, which reaches nearly to the eaves. Wurster also maximized the sense of space by using the outdoor porches as the house's only hallways, and by incorporating terraces into the body of the house. The dining and bedroom terraces were designed to be sheltered and comfortable places to relax in the sun or shade; as well, they were protected from the wind when the weather was less welcoming.

This project is an excellent example of how Wurster used simplification of detailing, uniformity of materials, and few defined thresholds to enlarge the architectural spaces. The L-shape of the main space gives the living and dining areas distinction without boundaries. The white tongue-and-groove pine boards "rubbed with a rotten stone for a light warm grey brown color" that finish all of the walls and ceilings—and even the interior doors of this space—also serve to tie the room to the uniformity and simplicity of the building's exterior siding and color.

This house is another example of Wurster's view that doing small things well is one of the of the architect's most important contributions.

opposite: The living room corner window looks west toward Point Lobos.

top: View toward the bedroom porch
left: The living and dining areas
right: View toward the terrace

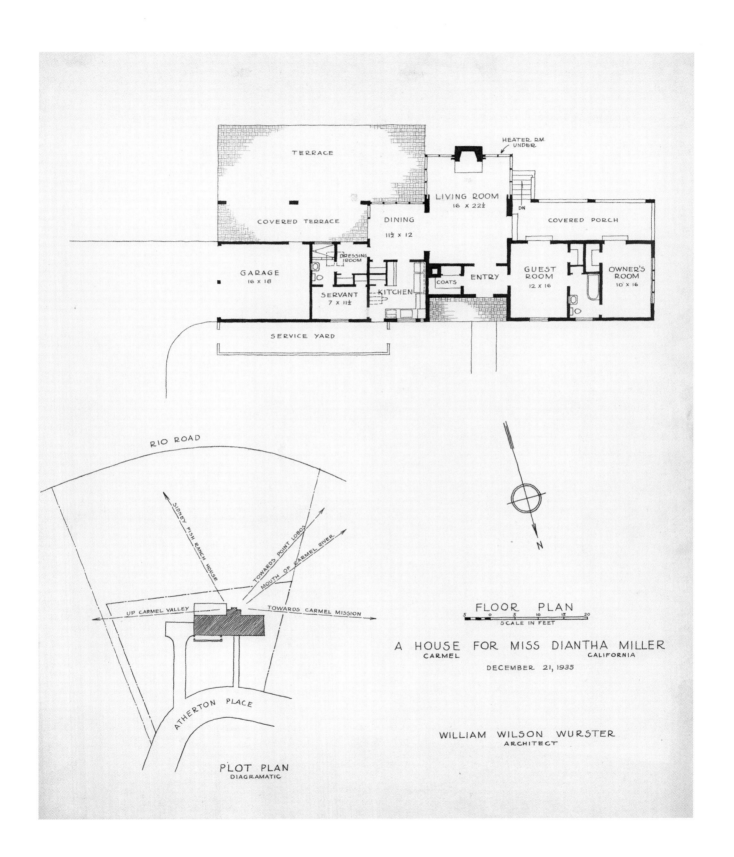

TERRACE

COVERED TERRACE

GARAGE
16 X 18

SERVANT
7 X 11½

DRESSING ROOM

KITCHEN

DINING
11½ X 12

LIVING ROOM
16 X 22½

HEATER RM.
UNDER

DN

COVERED PORCH

COATS

ENTRY

GUEST ROOM
12 X 16

OWNER'S ROOM
10 X 16

SERVICE YARD

RIO ROAD

SIDNEY PISH RANCH HOUSE

TOWARDS POINT LOBOS

MOUTH OF CARMEL RIVER

UP CARMEL VALLEY

TOWARDS CARMEL MISSION

ATHERTON PLACE

PLOT PLAN
DIAGRAMATIC

N

FLOOR PLAN
SCALE IN FEET

A HOUSE FOR MISS DIANTHA MILLER
CARMEL   CALIFORNIA
DECEMBER 21, 1935

WILLIAM WILSON WURSTER
ARCHITECT

The site and floor plan describes critical
environmental relationships.

opposite and above: The living room and terrace.
Wurster chose this color for the house to reflect the color of the sea and the sky.

above: The dining room and living room contain hidden pockets
built in the corner windows to store drapes.

The living room

Dondo House

Point Richmond, California

The 850-square-foot house was built to partially stand on the edge of the San Francisco Bay. The house, garage, and garden walls were constructed of prefabricated "underdown" block and the floors made of hollow brick tile for minimum upkeep.[10] The exterior materials were also the primary interior finishes. The wood-framed roof had a tar and gravel topcoat and the Dondos considered it a compromise as they wanted a concrete roof as well as walls. Employing the same materials inside and out made the modest interiors appear generous as the terrace with the same walls and floor finish functioned as an extension and as a room.

The windows were framed in redwood, painted at the exterior, and untreated inside. Where units were to be operable, steel casements were constructed and their frames embedded within a reveal of the wood frame. The cabinets and interior doors were made of marine grade plywood and waxed—with pulls made from the same material and laid out for function as well

as pattern design. Interior doors within the primary living space were clad in turquoise-stained canvas—so that every opening had the color of the outdoors (the Bay and the garden). All of the spaces focus either on the protected lushly landscaped courtyard or toward the dramatic view of the Bay which, at high tide, laps under the house and gives the house a distinct character of being "out to sea."

As the rooms are modest in size (though expansive from borrowed views) the combined quality of the natural light with the drama of the undulating water is very effective. It was a straightforward use of economical materials and allowed for Wurster's focus on expansiveness and freedom from maintenance and integration with the unique environmental opportunities of the specific location. This unique setting, blurring the boundary between dry and wet spaces at the water's edge, was also reflected in the delineation of a separate "cave" for the owner's racing shell and other aquatic recreation equipment.

opposite: The view to San Francisco

left: Toward the site for the yet-unbuilt Golden Gate Bridge
right, top: The barren landscape, boat cave, and scull
right, bottom: The living room
opposite, top: The house, from the courtyard
opposite, bottom: View from the shore

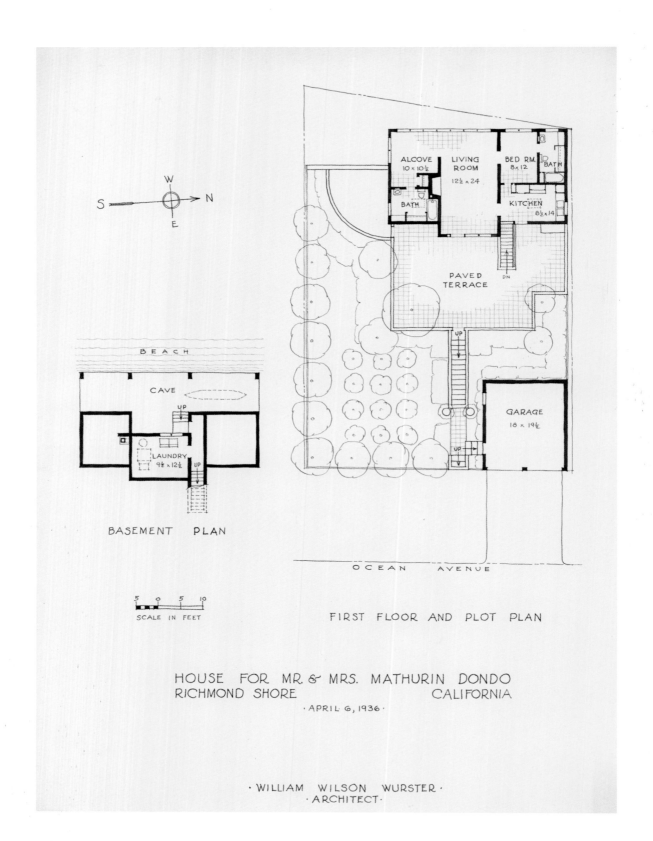

S — W — N — E (compass)

ALCOVE
10 × 10½

LIVING
ROOM
12½ × 24

BED RM.
8 × 12

BATH

BATH

KITCHEN
8½ × 14

PAVED
TERRACE

DN

UP

UP

GARAGE
18 × 19½

OCEAN   AVENUE

BEACH

CAVE

UP

LAUNDRY
9½ × 12½

UP

BASEMENT   PLAN

5 0 5 10
SCALE IN FEET

FIRST FLOOR AND PLOT PLAN

HOUSE FOR MR. & MRS. MATHURIN DONDO
RICHMOND SHORE   CALIFORNIA
· APRIL 6, 1936 ·

· WILLIAM   WILSON   WURSTER ·
· ARCHITECT ·

Site and floor plan

Views of the living room, top: toward the courtyard
bottom: toward the San Francisco Bay

top: View from living room toward bedroom
bottom: View from living room through the kitchen to the courtyard,
the built-in ceiling fixture provides diffused lighting to the entry area at night
opposite: Detail view of living room window

Jensen House

Berkeley, California

Built in a grove of redwoods and eucalyptus in the Berkeley hills, this house was designed as a rental unit for a contractor who had constructed many of Wurster's projects. It was designed to be a one-bedroom rental unit for a single resident— an interior designer and longtime colleague and friend of Wurster's was to be the tenant.[11] The project had the site limitation of preserving as many of the redwoods as possible while also allowing for some sunny exposures and fine, but restricted views of the San Francisco Bay.[12] The living and dining rooms' floor-to-ceiling windows and doors looked over a terrace to views of San Francisco, which effectively enlarged the small spaces. Furthering this effect, the terrace tile was carried through the living and dining rooms, visually linking the spaces. The bedrooms also shared the view, as did a large deck that doubled as a sleeping porch. The interior walls of the living-dining room were finished in white pine plywood and other rooms in solid white pine boards butted to reflect more natural light into the small rooms. The exterior was sided in bleached re-sawn red-wood boards. Built on the scale of a ship's cabin, it is another example of Wurster's designs that demonstrates his conviction that even the smallest of jobs require and deserve crafting to achieve architecture.

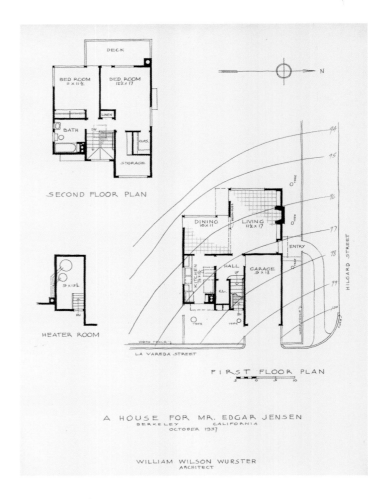

above: Site and floor plan
opposite, top and bottom: The generous
qualities of the living and dining area windows and doors

Hamill House

San Francisco, California

James Hamill was a close friend of Nora Kenyon, who had developed a four-plex of cottages on Bay Street in San Francisco just two years before. The Hamill family bought this site because it was adjacent to Kenyon's cottage development (see pages 100–105) and because its steep slope, considered unbuildable, made the price of the lot quite reasonable. In order for the interior rooms to have site lines above the multi-storied buildings across the street, the entry was set quite far back on the site (at the same level as Kenyon's). It took nearly a hundred steps to reach the modest front door.[13]

The main living spaces are on the second floor where the views northward are spectacular. This was achieved by putting only the entry and storage spaces on the lowest floor so that the entrance foyer actually occurred on the second floor after rising on the first staircase from the lower level. The second-floor foyer is flooded with natural light from the glazed curving staircase at the center of the house—"[the] glassed in stair on garden side was designed to brighten the entrance."[14] The stair also effectively brings light deep into the top floor with the use of internal windows along the hallway. Despite the bulk of the house and its tight configuration, the rooms that look into the garden do not have shadows cast onto their windows because the transparency of the staircase allows light to pass through it. On this tight lot with San Francisco's frequent foggy days, what might have been a dismal solution for a garden and an interior is actually quite light and successful. There is a more decidedly modern influence here with the sinuous staircase, and these lines are similar to the work Wurster was doing at the same time for the Benner family in Berkeley, which he referred to as "modern."

This glazed central stair system is a recurring theme throughout many of Wurster's houses as it successfully blends the indoor and outdoor spaces and brings light deep into a house. This house design was done just after Wurster's travels to Europe with Thomas and Elizabeth Church. The long balcony, which looked northward toward the Golden Gate, was used as an outdoor living space—it extended the feeling of the interior living and dining rooms to encompass spectacular views of San Francisco Bay, increasing the vitality of the hillside residence. "The north galleries gave a chance on good days to walk out to be part of the bay view."[15] As with nearly all of Wurster's homes, the siting, glazing, scale, and arrangement of the rooms allowed natural light to penetrate surprisingly deep into every room and created balanced illumination.

opposite: This garden view of the main curving staircase shows the continuous qualities of the horizontal alignments from window sill to stair wall to window mullion.

Early view of the front door and entry walk, a garden area now completely filled with an urban forest
which screens all but the upper bedroom balcony from public view.

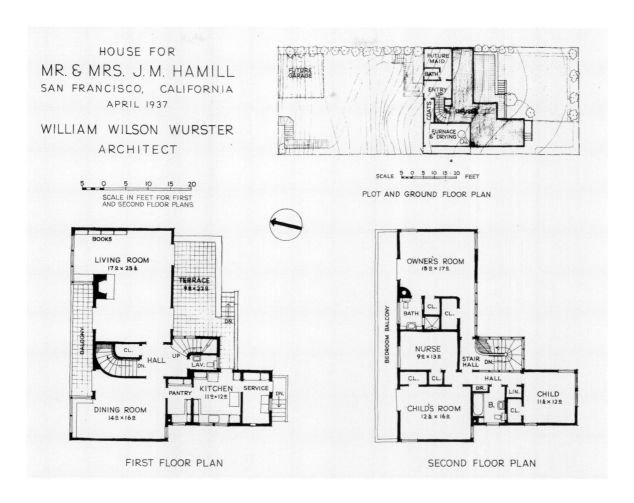

HOUSE FOR
MR. & MRS. J. M. HAMILL
SAN FRANCISCO, CALIFORNIA
APRIL 1937

WILLIAM WILSON WURSTER
ARCHITECT

SCALE IN FEET FOR FIRST
AND SECOND FLOOR PLANS

PLOT AND GROUND FLOOR PLAN

FIRST FLOOR PLAN

SECOND FLOOR PLAN

top: The floor and site plan show the steepness of the front yard relative to the flat garden in back.
bottom: The contrast of the private garden to the steep and closed approach of the public view

The garden terrace and stair

left: View toward the balcony, living room, and the distant San Francisco Bay
right: The main stair

above: The dining room and living room

The main stair

above and opposite: Views of the upper hall and stair. The window sills are aligned to
the curving stair guardrail as well as the interior translucent window.

[1937]

Mendenhall House

Palo Alto, California

This small house located on a flat suburban lot was striking because the clients wanted a 6-foot wall to enclose the entire property so that its front facade appeared to be a series of layered walls with just a modest horizontal plane to denote protection at the front door. As with many of Wurster's projects, all of the exterior materials were similar so there would be no distinction between house and enclosing wall—and in this case they were horizontal boards painted gray. Openings to the street were utilitarian and limited. In contrast, the interior spaces and the generous windows were arranged to open up entirely to the garden. The entire roof was a wall-screened terrace, which provided a private place for sunbathing and entertaining "free from the interruptions of the lower floor life."[17] The interiors were intended to be completely white—plaster interior walls and furnishings and bleached wood floors. Because of the specific complexities of the site and the needs of the client, what emerged was a very livable small house with the feeling of a much larger one. Wurster called it an "example of the use of intelligent planning to give spaciousness and dignity to a creatively small house."[18]

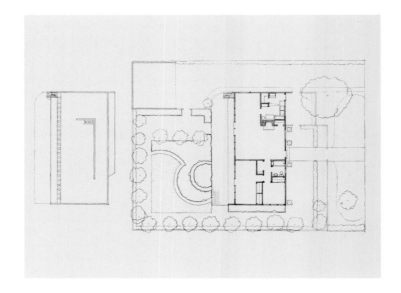

left: The screened sun-bathing roof porch
right: Site and floor plan

The efforts made to ensure absolute privacy for
the Mendenhalls and their guests.

Clark House

Aptos, California

"Built on the seashore, the structure rests on concrete piles. The house is of 'single board' construction—the walls being simply one thickness of boards placed vertically. Studding is entirely omitted. There are a few posts supporting beams over [the] head of large openings of [the] lower story, and at corners of [the] lower story. Other than this the entire structure—roof second floor and deck is held up only by the 1-inch thickness of boards. These boards are of redwood with tongued and grooved joints for weather tightness, with surface left rough."[19] The redwood exterior boards were left untreated because "redwood 'as is' is so darned beautiful [and] the white trim gives it a smart, alert look—fresh as any modern thing."[20]

Located on Monterey Bay, the central kitchen cave on the beach level could be enlarged to twice its size by pushing back the large barn-sliding doors that opened to the porch, making the two spaces a single unit. The intent was "To have it as different from the finished all-year-round place as possible—so that wet bathing suits, dogs, etc., could feel at home without any 'don'ts' or causing work."[21] The outdoor porch was flanked by a one-and-a-half-story-tall glazed sheltered sitting areas providing wind- and rain-protected spaces for enjoying life next to the ocean. "To give out of door shelter from wind—to emphasize the water by turning in from neighbors—In a word to make it the reverse side of the coin of daily living."[22] The bedrooms were kept small and were accessed only from an exterior staircase thereby freeing the main living space from through traffic. As with most of Wurster's small houses, the public rooms were generously scaled relative to the overall size of the house with the seamless transitions to outdoor spaces enhancing this effect.

opposite, top: View of the house from the beach
opposite, bottom: Exterior of house

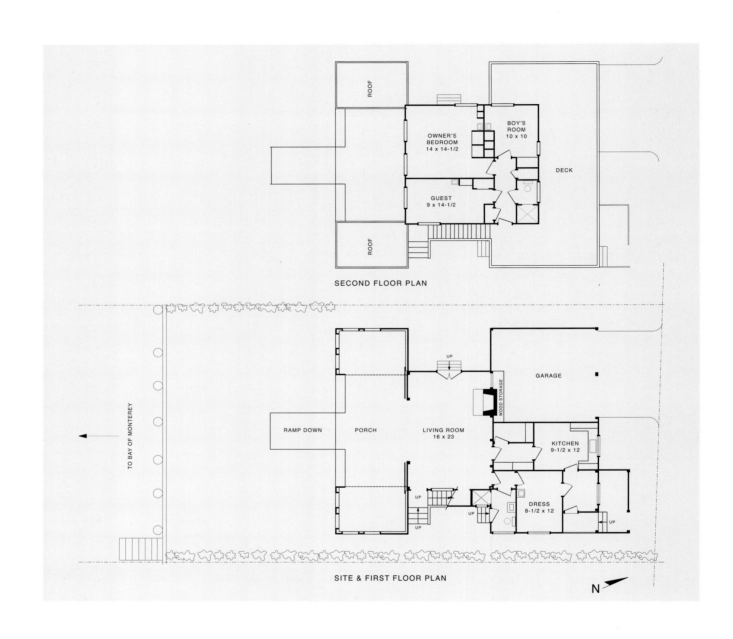

SECOND FLOOR PLAN

SITE & FIRST FLOOR PLAN

top: The floor and site plan show that the walls were built
with posts and single, flat boards

top: Living room
bottom: Looking south through
the glazed alcoves of the porch

Green Camp

Mount Diablo State Park, Walnut Creek area, California

Wurster designed an award-winning (*House Beautiful* Honorable Mention, 1941) weekend and summer retreat on the south slope of Mount Diablo, a large mountain that dominates the landscape of its surrounding valley. It was "located just a few hundred feet below the summit…with a grand outlook of the surrounding country."[23] The Green property was the only private land in the area as the rest of the mountain was a state park and protected open space.

The house was designed with a large outside room, the Big Porch, open to the surrounding terrain of rolling hills. It was originally planned as a structure with only gathering spaces—all of the bedrooms were to be tents assembled on a raised deck. The final design had two screened bunkrooms for the children and their visiting playmates. As with many of his projects, primary circulation was through a variety of partially protected outdoor spaces. The strong afternoon winds that dominated at this high elevation were mitigated by the jogged plan and also by the use of large sliding doors for shelter and for cooling. The hot, dry setting demanded protection from the sun, so Wurster carefully oriented the porch space to connect the living wing to the sleeping wing, providing maximum comfort throughout the year. Wurster viewed this house as an innovative solution.[24]

The house, which had a spread-out plan "in order to catch cooling breezes" had an exterior that was sided in horizontal 10-inch boards that were "rough treated with bleaching oil."[25] The interior walls were all finished in pine plywood. The floors, inside and out, were hollow clay tiles set on a concrete slab. The house was designed to be "free from the restrictions of city living as regards room, furnishings and free access to out of doors."[26]

opposite, top: The camp and the surrounding landscape of Mount Diablo
opposite, bottom: The entrance shelter through the large sliding doors to the
big porch and the valley view beyond

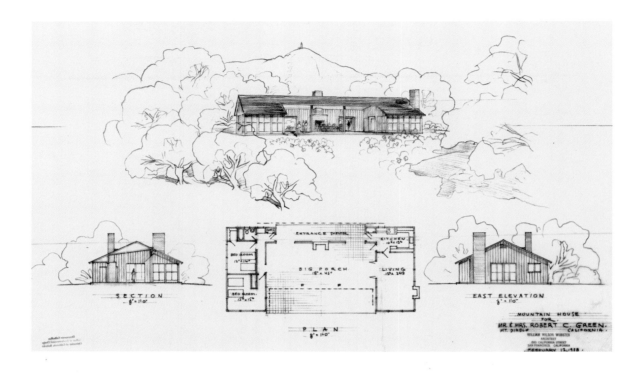

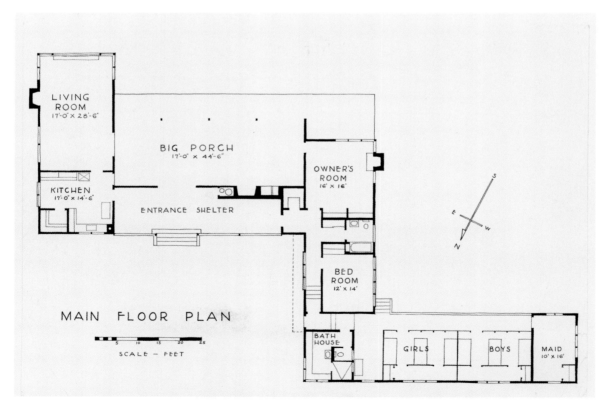

top: Early design sketches
bottom: This floor plan shows the evolution of the design from the
gable-roofed massing to the more varied plan and roof lines.

View of the walkway and the screened boys' and girls' bunkrooms

above: The big porch area, showing the varied ways to enjoy the space
opposite: From the entrance shelter toward the living room

1939

—

1963

THE LATE ERA

Beginning with the San Francisco World's Fair and
extending until his death, William Wurster refined his work
into a set of solutions that maintained his early interest
in responding to unique qualities of a site in a way that was
minimal enough to allow for the client's full expression.

Gerbode House

San Francisco, California

The large, formal city house that Wurster designed in the hills of San Francisco's Pacific Heights neighborhood is organized around a terrace that looks south and east toward the financial district and across the San Francisco Bay toward Berkeley. The house appeared both classical and undeniably modern.

Wurster's design inherited a large lot with an existing enclosing wall from a previously demolished estate. The footprint of the house is not overly large given its context, and yet by spreading the plan into a thin L, the house presents a majestic presence on the corner lot in this prestigious neighborhood. In order to maximize the interior spaces, access to natural light, and magnificent views, the entry was placed surprisingly close to the sidewalk and the enclosing wall. The main public rooms span the width of the building and because there are generous openings between the rooms, each room has natural light from at least three sides.

The entry, nearly the largest space in the house, is anchored by a magnificent staircase that continues Wurster's design ideas of well-lit, curving staircases to bring light into the middle of the house and to make the element a focal point.

Given its grand Victorian and neo-classical neighbors of the time, this house was quite a departure for the community.[1]

above: Sketches of the exterior and the staircase
opposite, top: The sheltered entry, from the street corner
opposite, bottom: The terrace view toward the dining and living room

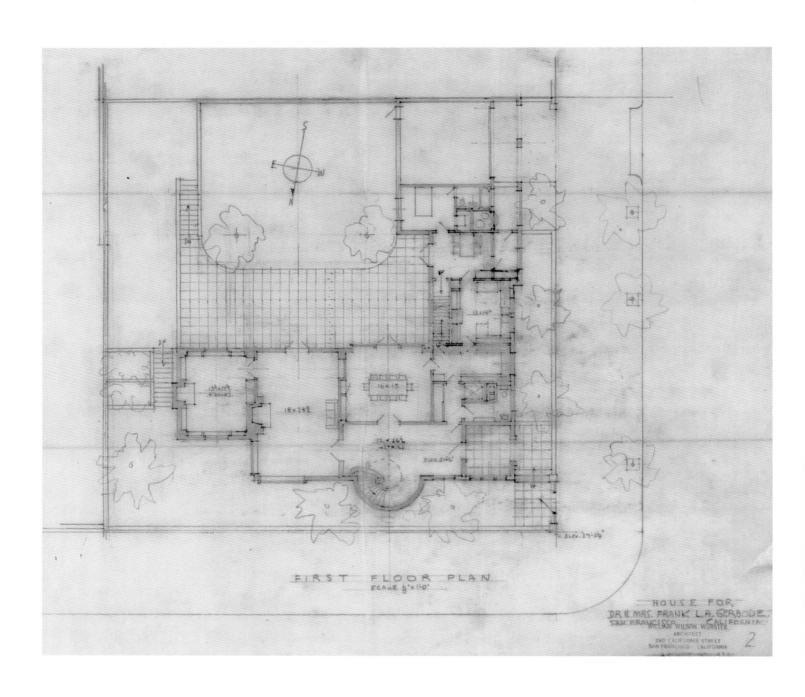

FIRST FLOOR PLAN
SCALE ⅛"=1'-0"

HOUSE FOR,
DR & MRS. FRANK L.A. GERBODE
SAN FRANCISCO   CALIFORNIA
WILLIAM WILSON WURSTER
ARCHITECT
260 CALIFORNIA STREET
SAN FRANCISCO CALIFORNIA

2

The design sketch of the approved floor plan shows the proximity of
the house to the preexisting stone wall.

left: View of the large curving window at the main stairway
right: Main stair in entry hall

Grover House

San Francisco, California

Wurster was hired as the architect for this house just as he was completing the Gerbode House across the street. The clients chose the lot in this very exclusive neighborhood because, though it was small, it had breathtaking views toward the Golden Gate, San Francisco Bay, and Mount Tamalpias in the Marin Headlands at the rear and north of the property. These views were to be protected by a height easement over the adjacent parcel. The lot was a traditional San Francisco rowhouse proportion, atypical for this particular neighborhood, approximately 25-feet wide and 100-feet deep. These small lots were laid out with the intention that the houses would share side-yard walls without openings, and that the primary sources of daylight would occur at the short ends of the lot. Wurster intended to maximize access to natural light while also providing indoor to outdoor relationships that relate to the restrictions and opportunities. Given the small size of the lot, he provided a solution that was considered quite unusual at the time. Despite the fact that *Architectural Forum* described it as having a "bland functional front," the journal found the house to be quite appealing in its hidden charm.[2]

The client wanted a house that had the ease and scale of apartment living but also some sense of "country living."[3] Wurster's design placed the living spaces "as close to the view as possible" as "northern gardens are not livable in this climate."[4] The desired views are at the rear end of the lot, contrary to a typical layout as it is far from the entrance. Instead of the traditional approach of embedding the garage in the house, Wurster separated it "so as to not waste valuable space

on the driveway."[5] By setting the garage below grade, he was able to retain and level the sloping space between the garage and the house and thereby create a sheltered sunny garden. It was considered a "country like setting" because of its complete privacy; since future houses would predictably present solid walls to it, it would likely retain its privacy over time, "so that on any sunny day lunch could be taken in the garden in warmth and privacy."[6] As with so many of his other houses, by breaking the house into two structures linked by a covered passageway, Wurster allowed each room more opportunities for balanced natural light and created critical space out of the outdoor room. There was a decision to give the view to the living room and the garden to the dining room. This created an unusual plan, placing the kitchen and dining room on the ground floor and the living room two stories above. To facilitate a natural flow, the curvaceous stairways are well lit by light wells that bring daylight into the central halls. Additionally, Wurster enlarged the doors and used glass doors on the interior and exterior to encourage circulation.

The third-floor living room has dramatic unobstructed views north and east. Additionally, through large French doors and across a wind-sheltered deck, it has views and daylight from the south. The deck is large enough to have complete privacy and has shelter enough from an extended eave line that its views can be enjoyed even in the rain. As with many of his houses at the time, Wurster preferred to use simple redwood. For the Grover House he painted the exterior wood siding and trim, except at the third-floor deck with its

opposite: View of the entry passage, the garden, and dining room doors on the right

enclosing walls, which he left natural to reduce glare and to absorb more warmth from the sun.

The garden, designed in collaboration with Thomas Church, is successful not only because it is the center of circulation, but also because the garage was built into the slope, allowing the southern sun to penetrate and reflect off the south-facing taller wall of the main rooms.

In response to the unusually simple material choices for a house located in a neighborhood of ornate mansions, Wurster wrote a reflection on his methodology which accompanied his submission to *Architectural Forum*: "It was decided to do it as direct as an old shoe—with not one thing applied as ornament. This has resulted in a

severity, which is a bit out of key with the neighborhood, but I believe sympathetic buildings placed alongside will care for this. It seems to economy—ease of living—and the movement and privacy in house and garden comparable to a country place and this is what we wanted."[7]

The ingenuity of the plan for this house was further developed by Wurster in several projects that followed—most notably in the nearby Coleman House (pages 186–189), built twenty years later.

Wurster was finishing the Grover House just as he moved east with his wife Catherine in 1941, and in 1949, just as Wurster was returning to California, the Grovers commissioned Wurster to build another house for them in Woodside.

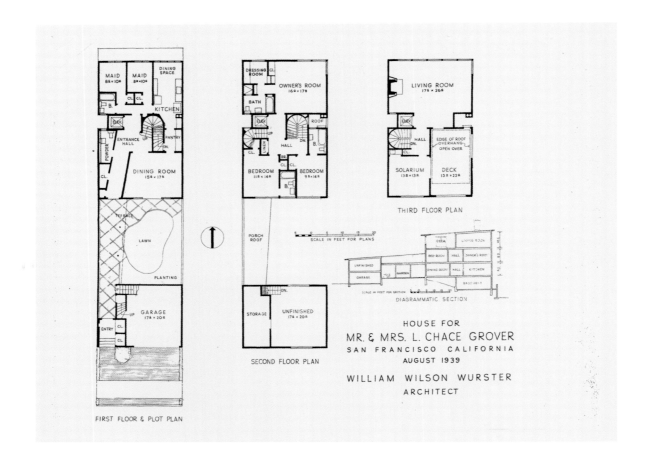

The floor plans and building section show the complicated solution for this stacked city house.

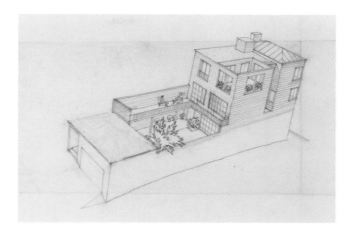

top left: View into the garden from the bedroom over the garage
top right: Concept sketch
bottom: The view from the third-floor living room's sheltered roof deck

above: The dining room and garden
opposite: View of the main rooms of the house from the garden. The original roof deck
(upper-right corner) was in-filled to make a sunroom.

Chickering House

Woodside, California

Wurster worked on at least nine commissions over twenty-five years for the Chickering family. In this summerhouse Wurster incorporated an example of what he referred to in the office and with clients as "a room with no name"; here it takes the form of a spacious central lanai that provides a link between the private bedrooms and public rooms. Built with similar details as the exterior, 1-by-10-foot painted, rough-sawn redwood boards, rather than the plaster finish of the rest of the house, it serves as a transition space between the entrance porch, gardens, and living spaces. Wurster noted: "There was a desire for an indoor-outdoor room [which] was met by the Lanai with great sliding glass doors."[8]

Whether its large, south-facing glass panels, which spanned the entire length of the 38-foot-long space, are opened or closed, this multipurpose room relates to the terraces and gardens in a relaxed and inviting way. The lanai took away the need for a living room in this tranquil setting, and instead a large study with an oversized pocket door to the patio was provided. The landscape, designed in collaboration with Thomas Church, maintained the large oak for shade from the hot summer sun on the south-facing lanai and concrete patio. Wurster's design for this room again illustrates his unique understanding of the elements required to create a room for fluid needs.

above, left: View of the courtyard, looking into the lanai
above, right: The corner window and doors at the study
opposite, top: The lanai
opposite, bottom: Site and floor plan

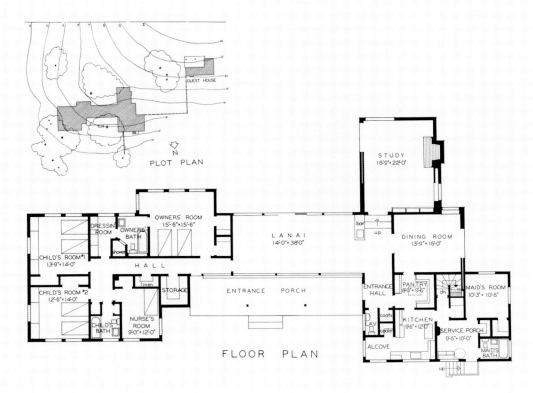

PLOT PLAN

GUEST HOUSE

N

STUDY
16'-9" x 22'-0"

OWNERS' ROOM
15'-6" x 15'-6"

DRESSING
ROOM

OWNERS'
BATH

shower

LANAI
14'-0" x 38'-0"

bar

up

DINING ROOM
13'-9" x 16'-0"

CHILD'S ROOM #1
13'-9" x 14'-0"

HALL

CHILD'S ROOM #2
12'-6" x 14'-0"

linen

STORAGE

CHILD'S
BATH

NURSE'S
ROOM
9'-0" x 12'-0"

ENTRANCE PORCH

ENTRANCE
HALL

PANTRY
8'-0" x 9'-6"

coats

LAV

cooler

KITCHEN
9'-6" x 12'-0"

ALCOVE

dn

MAID'S ROOM
10'-3" x 10'-6"

SERVICE PORCH
9'-6" x 10'-0"

MAID'S
BATH

up

FLOOR PLAN

S. Pope House

Lafayette, California

Located on the hillside of an inland valley east of San Francisco, this house had a structural system that was in large part a response to the conditions of the site. The protected coastal valley enjoyed warm summers as well as evenings that were cooled by strong, foggy breezes headed from San Francisco and Berkeley, what the client called the "wind which occurs at the sunny edges of fog banks."[9] Along with the climate variables, the rural grassland setting was vulnerable to wildfires.[10]

The Popes called this project the "playhouse of their middle life" as it was a place for them to cultivate their gardens and for Jeanne Pope to use her loom.[11] "Let the spirit of the playhouse be free—and let its materials be the most flexible possible," they requested.[12] The house was to be designed to shut out the world, especially on the weekends. Pope did not "want to look out at the world," rather, he wrote, "I want to get away from it—get shielded behind something—huddle in a court....I want to be protected from the elements—and want to create my own concept of beauty within the confines of the land on which I live."[13]

The Popes sought Wurster for this project because "it is the occasional streak of pure inspiration in your designs that [we] covet."[14] Wurster favored new materials and building techniques, but never for their own sake; in this house he responded to the setting by using underdown block and aluminum sheathing on the exterior, and unfinished plywood and hollow clay floor tiles with the unfinished block on the interior.[15] Wurster was encouraged to use unusual

materials by the client: "The sheer impertinence about the corrugated iron won our complete approval too....It's a lovely medium—both for color and form....I watched a shed in the morning light the vertical shadows were beautiful [sic]. It has great possibilities...if we can use long windowless masses of it...the scale of the corrugations must be as big as possible."[16] The client in fact encouraged a stripped-down, almost elemental, overall solution: "this is to be extremely simple—and as temporary as the fair."[17]

The interior and exterior spaces were quite similar. As with many of his projects, the distinction between wall and house and interior and exterior were not a hard boundary. The flooring and the wall of the living room area continued uninterrupted to a sheltered terrace and was divided only by a minimally mullioned wall of glass. The Douglas fir ceiling of the house extended to the ceiling of the atrium. The fireplace in the atrium reflects the fireplace in the living room.

The overall plan was derived by the relationship of the Popes' lives to a courtyard and adjacent garden. The interior courtyard in plan was also an open-air entrance that became a large outdoor space for lounging, dining, or playing. Thrilled after an inspirational design session with Wurster, Saxton Pope wrote: "[We] felt that raising the atrium out of the utilitarian class and making it the 'heart of the home' was one of those unexpected flashes of yours...you fuse necessity and the impossible dream into extremely fine metals."[18] The space could be opened to the rolling hills and cooling breezes or closed for privacy and shelter from the environment, while simultaneously serving

opposite: The interior atrium

as a central corridor. The large, 40-by-40-foot atrium had a large diameter opening that was not placed symmetrically over the symmetrical roof framing. The opening was intentionally positioned to make it as large as possible while also protecting the primary circulation to the greatest degree, which was between the garage and the front door.

The front wall was sheathed in corrugated steel and it extended and curved away from the basic rectangle of the house in order to screen garage doors, and direct arrivals toward an entry area that was otherwise very simply defined. A similar wall extension at the living room directed the views west and south toward the best view.

This house was a mature version of how Wurster strived to design sheltered outdoor spaces with similar details and materials as the interior rooms, blurring the distinctions between them—making indoor-outdoor spaces that centered on the life of a home.

top: The ribbon of windows along the bedroom and kitchen wing's north-facing facade
bottom: View of the front entry court whose curved wall leads to the garage entry

top: The atrium, from the private garden
bottom: The secluded front entry area

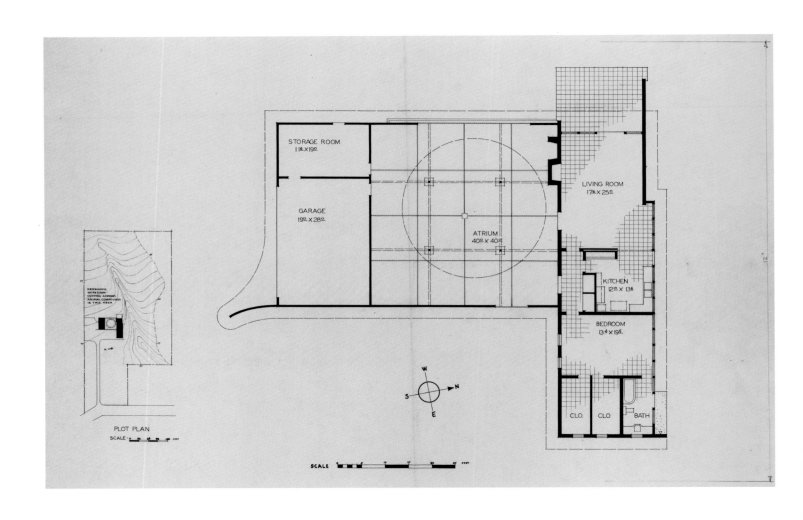

STORAGE ROOM
11⁶ x 19⁰

GARAGE
19⁰ x 28⁰

ATRIUM
40⁰ x 40⁰

LIVING ROOM
17⁶ x 25⁰

KITCHEN
12⁰ x 13⁶

BEDROOM
13⁶ x 19⁶

CLO.   CLO.   BATH

GREENHOUSE
WORK ROOM
CUTTING GARDENS
ANIMAL COMPOUNDS
IN THIS AREA

PLOT PLAN
SCALE

SCALE

above: Site and floor plan
opposite, top: The living room
opposite, bottom: Across the living room, toward the kitchen area

Wolski House

San Francisco, California

Built for two musicians on one of San Francisco's traditionally small lots, a mere 25 feet wide, this intimate townhouse has no prominent views. The entry is neatly tucked in off the street and accessed by passing under the front, two-story portion of the house. Originally designed as two discrete structures, the entry area eventually became an interior hall. A nod to the original intent of an entry breezeway can be seen in the modestly sloped ceiling that echoes the actual framing of the entry eaves. Extended rafters on the exterior emphasize this line.

The house has a large living room (15 by 30 feet) that opens onto a quiet, sunny south courtyard and was designed to double as a studio for piano lessons. Essentially a one-bedroom house, the second bedroom (7 by 20 feet) is the practice studio for William Wolski, the concert master and first violist for the San Francisco Symphony.

The living/dining/piano room and entry, with 12-foot-tall ceilings, serves as a railing for the upper floor's south bedroom terrace. The bedroom terrace allows for clerestories into these main floor rooms. The main rooms were all detailed without trim except for a modest crown and shoe mold. The walls, originally clad all in plywood, were replaced by a sympathetic remodel in 2008 which used vertical-grain fir plywood as an appropriate substitute.

The combination of large windows and doors without perceivable headers, clerestories, skylights, tall ceilings, and large interior doorways allows natural light to flood the spaces making a particularly small house feel generous and gracious.

opposite: View from the secluded front entry area back toward the street

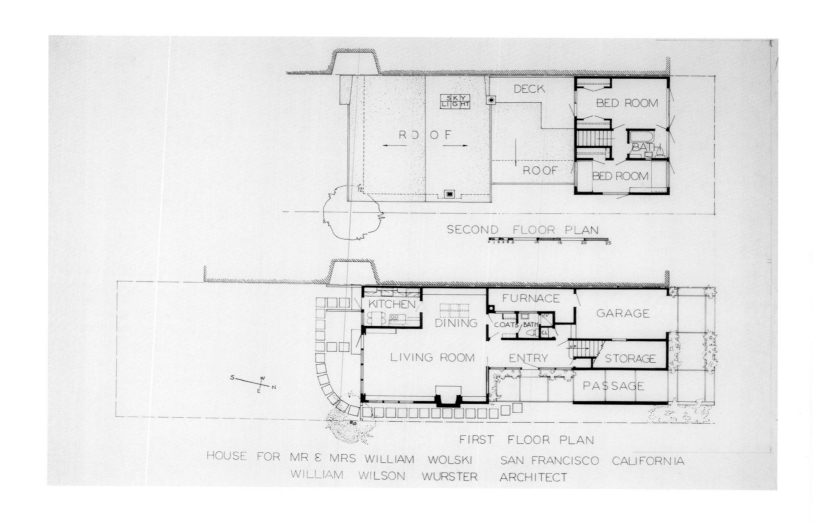

SECOND FLOOR PLAN

FIRST FLOOR PLAN

HOUSE FOR MR & MRS WILLIAM WOLSKI   SAN FRANCISCO CALIFORNIA
WILLIAM WILSON WURSTER   ARCHITECT

above: Site and floor plan
opposite, top: The entry area, accessed from a walkway tucked under the second floor
opposite, bottom: The back patio, with a sympathetic addition on the left

above: Front door and entry corridor
opposite: View from the living room toward entry corridor

above: The living room and dining areas

above: The living room, patio,
recently remodeled kitchen, and additional bedroom
overleaf: Living room

Walters House

San Francisco, California

In 1949, just before Wurster returned to the West Coast after a seven-year sojourn on the East Coast, he was asked to design this house for a seventy-year-old widowed bookbinder and local socialite, Florence Walters. Referred to Wurster by her good friend Elizabeth Church, she wanted a gracious home that suited her needs for exhibiting her five-thousand-volume book collection, her bookbinding studio, and a large and gracious area for entertaining.[19] Walters had enjoyed living in a grand Victorian house and, having been raised at the turn of the century, also enjoyed traditional amenities. This house, while a departure from the language of the nineteenth century, has gracious private amenities in its detailing and the articulation of its public space, including quarters for three servants.

The house is located on a steep and narrow north-facing site with magnificent views over Fisherman's Wharf toward Alcatraz and Angel islands. The house is a literal translation of the architectural language of the ferryboats that crisscross in front of the expansive windows of the main space.

Entered from a concrete ramp through a modest gangway-style gate, the exterior walls are kept low and roof pitches flat so that the Bay view can be glimpsed over the assembly. The modest scale of the entry is unimposing and inviting despite the lack of windows into the interior. The front entry court and gangway has a wind-sheltering, translucent glazed wall with a single, clear glass pane that frames a distant view to open up the confinement of the walled space.

The narrow and long interior entry hall, designed to exhibit the book collection, is an extension of the entry gangway. With ceilings over 10 feet tall, its walls are sheathed in teak decking. This, together with the high porthole-like windows, firmly established the ferryboat motif.

Like the entry hall, the dining room, which is a continuation of the entry, has no views of its own. Despite this, the room has abundant daylight from two sides: to the east through the windows it borrows from the living area and, dramatically, toward the west, where a hidden clerestory extends the width of the dining area, successfully washing the decking-clad wall with indirect eastern light.

Half of the living room area is glazed from floor to ceiling in panels that are similar in scale and proportion to the plywood siding that sheaths the exterior. The living area is the only part of the contiguous assembly of the entry/dining/living area that has views to the outside. This creates a powerful experience of an already awe-inspiring view. The public space reflects the new age in their interpretation of the "modern" way to live.

The exterior is intentionally modest and, appropriate to the postwar period and Wurster's aesthetics, clad in the plywood easily available at the time. The building continues Wurster's tradition of using easily obtained materials and local building skills to create architecture. The simple gangways that wrap the east and north glazed facades ingeniously provide transparent protection so that views are always available, while also providing an outside balcony experience of the dramatic setting from 30 feet above grade.

opposite: The narrow and tall entry hall, designed to be the library, has high clerestory windows reminiscent of portholes.

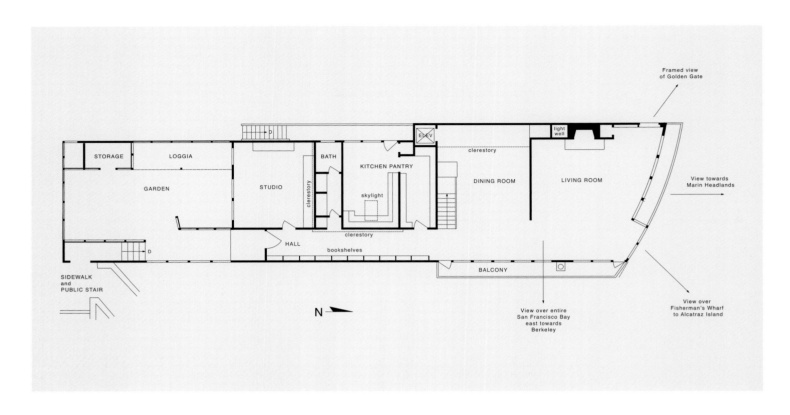

STORAGE

LOGGIA

Framed view
of Golden Gate

ELEV

light
well

GARDEN

STUDIO

BATH

KITCHEN PANTRY

clerestory

DINING ROOM

LIVING ROOM

View towards
Marin Headlands

clerestory

skylight

clerestory

SIDEWALK
and
PUBLIC STAIR

D

HALL

bookshelves

BALCONY

View over
Fisherman's Wharf
to Alcatraz Island

N

View over entire
San Francisco Bay
east towards
Berkeley

top: Floor plan
bottom: The ferryboat house

top: The entry gangway
bottom: The wind-sheltered garden with direct access to the owner's bookbindery

left: Views of the front door from inside and out explain the gangway quality of the entry.
right: The single panel of clear glass provides a framed view of the San Francisco Bay.
opposite: The large windows in this sitting area open directly.
overleaf: The living room looks north, with the Golden Gate to the west and
the campanile of Berkeley's campus in the east.

Heller House

North Lake Tahoe, Nevada

Lake Tahoe, encircled by the Sierra Nevada mountain range, sits astride the California-Nevada border at an elevation of approximately 6,000 feet. The Heller House, on Cascade Beach in Crystal Bay, lay at its northeast end and looked south across its length to the snowcapped range headed by Mount Talac. Long a sacred Native American site, it has become a mountain resort community enjoyed by many Californian families.

Sheltered from a nearby highway by a bluff, the house was built with large granite boulders quarried from nearby Mt. Rose. The plan was designed as two rectangular enclosures covered by one steeply pitched roof. Between the enclosures was a breezeway that could be easily opened up at either end by its two pairs of 9-foot pocket doors.

Stone that surfaced the hardscape outside the house also finished the breezeway floor, effectively bringing the outside in. The house, designed as an extended family retreat for a couple and the families of their three grown children, was divided between an entertainment and dormitory area.

Just after the house's completion Wurster reflected, "It was my endeavor to make it a direct contrast to neat city living. To make undue tidiness neither possible nor desired."[20] The rooms were laid out so that they spanned the width of the houses, not only allowing for direct access and views to the beach, but also providing respite from the heat and glare with a view to the green of the forest behind. "It was to be as casual as an old hat."[21]

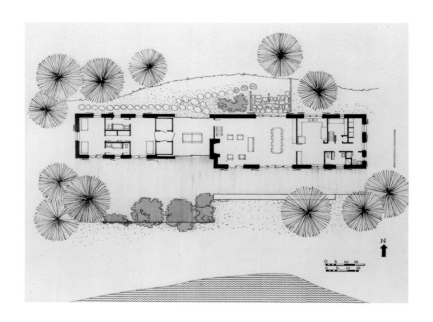

above: Site and floor plan
opposite, top: View from Lake Tahoe. The large doors would
open to allow for an expansive connection between the inside and out.
opposite, bottom: View from the forest behind the house

Coleman House

San Francisco, California

This five-story house had a two-story glazed gallery that encircled a garden atrium designed by Thomas Church. The atrium formed an essential light court and hallway that linked the interior spaces and the landscape. Expansive views to the north from the living room captured the stunning natural features of the Golden Gate and the entire San Francisco Bay Area.

One can see the roots of this design in Wurster's earliest work. This house had generously scaled rooms that related primarily to the distant views and the intimate landscape but not formally to each other. The focus of this house was the exposure of the occupants and visitors to the immensity of the setting. The boldness of the courtyard and its staircase from both outside and within was necessary to stand up to the magnificence of the views across the San Francisco Bay to the Golden Gate. The staircase was the point of reference for navigating the unusual plan. All of this natural and manufactured beauty was screened from the street by a modest facade, which told nothing of the story within. All of the rooms of importance were stacked one on top of the other and arranged without regard for convenience of service so that each had its own direct visual connection to the San Francisco Bay. This was carried to the lowest (basement) level where a narrow interior lap pool ran the length of the view.[22]

above: The stairwell and atrium
opposite: The atrium of the glazed stair

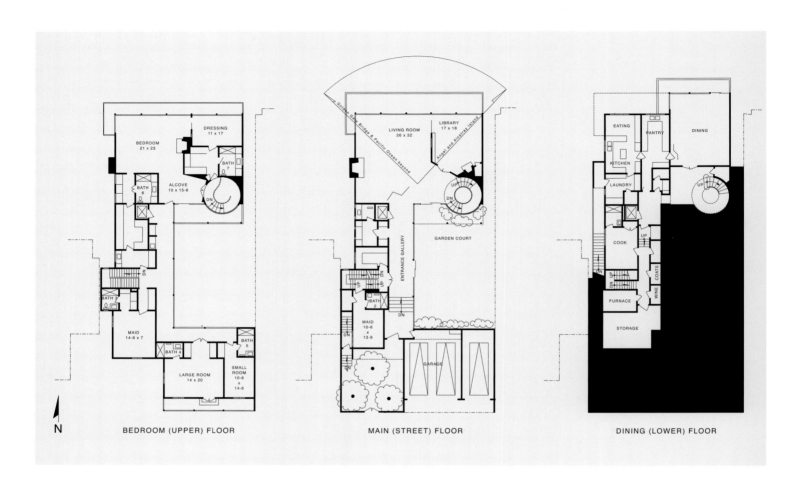

BEDROOM (UPPER) FLOOR

- BEDROOM 21 x 23
- DRESSING 11 x 17
- BATH 7
- ALCOVE 10 x 15-6
- BATH 6
- DN
- BATH 3
- MAID 14-6 x 7
- BATH 4
- BATH 5
- LARGE ROOM 14 x 20
- SMALL ROOM 10-6 x 14-6

MAIN (STREET) FLOOR

- LIVING ROOM 26 x 32
- LIBRARY 17 x 18
- Golden Gate Bridge & Pacific Ocean beyond
- Angel and Alcatraz Island
- UP
- DN
- ENTRANCE GALLERY
- GARDEN COURT
- UP DN
- BATH 2
- DN
- MAID 10-6 x 13-9
- DN
- GARAGE

DINING (LOWER) FLOOR

- EATING
- PANTRY
- DINING
- KITCHEN
- LAUNDRY
- UP
- COOK
- UP
- DN UP
- WINE
- COATS
- FURNACE
- STORAGE

N

2850

top: Floor plans
bottom: View from the street
opposite: Night view of the atrium and stair

G. Pope House

El Peco Ranch, Madera, California

Built on a thoroughbred horse-breeding farm for a family for whom Wurster had built a home some twenty years before, in Hillsborough, this adobe house was credited with influence from the Sanchez Adobe in Ion, California.[23] The family continued to spend much of the year in their Hillsborough home, using this house primarily as a weekend and summer base for their children and for raising world-class racehorses.

The house is a successful modern abstraction of the traditional adobes of early California. With its broad metal roof and simple supports, it was also quite similar to the hay sheds that dot the wide-open landscape of California's Central Valley. The main living areas occupied the upper of two floors and spanned the entire width of the building. The summers are quite hot and dry and there was relief found under the large, covered wraparound veranda. By occupying the second level, the veranda and main living spaces caught the afternoon's cooling breezes. The veranda had two screened porches (one more formal than the other) and one could therefore always find a shady,

protected place to relax. From the porch the views extended across horse paddocks and manicured gardens by Thomas Church toward orchards and the sweeping open spaces of the valley.

Wurster used the natural insulating characteristics of adobe for the main rectangular form of the house. Simple, large double-hung windows were deep set into flared openings, which created natural sitting places throughout the house. The second-floor ceilings are 12 feet high (8 feet on the lower level) and the significant doors were kept tall and wide. The interior ceilings and walls were all sheathed in re-sawn wood.[24] The interior doors of minor importance (closets, bathrooms, bedrooms) were also sheathed in wood to appear blind and kept to a traditional size to focus attention on more important spaces and circulation.

Upon its completion, it was said about the house: "Although it continues and frankly recognizes the tradition of the great house on the working farm, this house derives from the Wurster conviction, not from any style, period or region."[25]

opposite, top: The ramped entry to the house
opposite, bottom: The garden, from the former polo field

An exterior view toward the screened sitting room

The screened sitting room looks out over the racehorse paddocks.

opposite: The entry hall, like the entire house, has exterior adobe walls and
interior walls finished in wood from the family's mills.
left: The entry hall has a view to the screened porch and living room.
The less important doors are clad in siding and built to be blind.
right: The screened porch and the paddocks beyond, since replaced by orchards

left: The dining room with a combination of adobe and wood clad walls
right: The ground level recreation and service bedrooms had a lower ceiling than the
main level above in order to give it a closer connection to the surrounding landscape.
opposite: The main stair was built from a walnut tree on the family's land.

[1957]

W. Henderson House

Hillsborough, California

This house is an example of Wurster's ability to achieve the stateliness of a large formal house with a modest amount of floor area. His first house for this family was designed nearly twenty-five years earlier and was much more traditional in its execution. For this project, the simplicity of the forms belies the size of the house, which balances a formal plan with ample public rooms against an informal relationship between indoors and out. This house is located in a large open landscape where the Hendersons wished to enjoy weekends, entertain a number of friends, and have ample and appropriate space to exhibit their art collection.

Despite the overall proportions of the house—117-feet-by-more-than-80-feet—the large, central, open-air atrium (approximately 27-feet-by 22-feet) provides a light-filled circulation center to the house. All rooms are entered from the glazed central gallery around the atrium and extend to the exterior gardens. Each room employs different methods to allow for ample and balanced natural light. The simplicity of the detailing of materials—the polished terrazzo on the gallery floor (similar in pattern to the gravel of the central atrium) and the teak-clad walls in the dining and living rooms, for example—are a more informal response than a house of this caliber would usually have. The house

is surrounded by Thomas Church gardens and each side of the house has distinct outside spaces, landscaping, views, and use. The most notable and important outdoor room is the large south-facing living porch (entered from the glazed gallery) that overlooks the dramatic pool and views beyond.

The central atrium is a late-career example of Wurster's earliest design principles: using a central outdoor space as the primary orienting space of the house. In this case, the atrium was landscaped to be looked at more than inhabited. It was designed to bring indirect light into what was essentially an art gallery space. The circulating "glazed gallery" is deep enough and tall enough (11 feet) to prevent direct daylight from reaching the collection that hang on the walls. The atrium's structural system is kept to a minimum so all of the art can be seen and so the views to the garden are always visible.

In plan, the private bedrooms are located a the front of the house and the rhythm of their overlarge bay windows along that facade create a sophisticated accentuation of an otherwise subtle entry. This allows the entertaining rooms, with their simple floor-to-ceiling double-hung windows, to have the primary enjoyment of the gardens.

opposite: The large-scaled bedroom bays flank the
discrete entryway along the entrance drive.

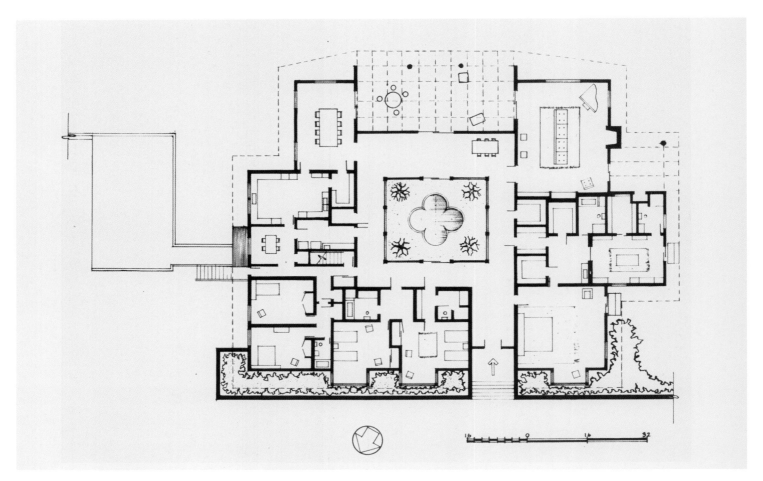

top: Site and floor plan
bottom: The large porch terrace overlooks the pool and gardens.
opposite, top: Exterior view of the eleven-foot-tall windows within all the rooms
opposite, bottom: The atrium
overleaf: View from the gardens toward the big porch shows the glow of the atrium beyond

Baer House

Big Sur, California

Morley Baer and his wife, Frances, were long-time colleagues and friends of the Wursters. Catherine and Bill (as he was often called in his later years) had, in fact, sold the Baers their Rudolf Schindler house on Greenwood Commons in Berkeley, in 1952, when the Wursters purchased the nearby house of Sarah Gregory. Morley Baer worked closely with Wurster, photographing much of the Wurster, Bernardi & Emmons work in the 1950s and 1960s. Baer's first photographic passion was the California coastline between Carmel and Big Sur, and inspired by Edward Weston's work, he wanted to return to the coast on a more permanent basis. With generous funds from a fortuitous sale, the Baers bought a pristine site south of Carmel near Big Sur at Garrapata Creek. The purchase of the property came with an agreement to keep any structure sheltered from the view of a neighbor.

The house was to "look like it grew out of the ground and that it was made from the materials of the surrounding landscape. It was to be like a stone barn, simple and rough."[26] The view was sited to face north and screened and sheltered by a rocky saddle to the south. To the north were dramatic views of Garrapata Creek beach and to Sobranes Point and the mountain range between. Baer photographed this landscape throughout his career and he wanted unfettered access to it. The stone for the house—a local rock known as Del Monte Granite used primarily for driveways and retaining walls at the time—was chosen to blend in and become part of the landscape. It was to be like the rock of the adjacent saddle.

At its earliest stages the house was designed to be "one room under one roof."[27] It eventually evolved into a large double-height living room which descended via a few generous steps, to the kitchen. Above the kitchen was a loft for sleeping.

The interior of the living room was sided in wood and painted white. The large 14-by-14-foot glass and mullion window extended from floor to plate, its view mirroring Baer's black and white photographs hanging on the adjacent walls. The experience of the ever-changing weather conditions was awe-inspiring. The scale of the main room was called "audacious" for the time, but was a comforting contrast to the stone walls and low-timbered ceiling of the kitchen, which also served as the entry.[28]

top: The front of the house, including the large glazed window,
which frames the photographer's view of the landscape
left: The wind-protected side of the house enjoys an intimate view of the saddle.
right: An example of the framed views inside the house
opposite: A framed view through the big room window

Acknowledgments

Given the spread of time this project took and the enthusiasm that many have for William Wilson Wurster, the list of the many able colleagues and friends that assisted us can never be complete. But in an effort to do so, let us say:

Richard Peters was originally introduced to the work of Wurster by the architect and professor, Vernon DeMars. A dear friend of Wurster and his family, DeMars recruited Dick when he was still a graduate student to join the legion of groundbreaking professionals at Berkeley's Department of Architecture. Under the leadership of Wurster, this collaboration created the College of Environmental Design, and taught legions of students in a new way that changed the nature of architectural education and architecture itself.

Wurster's long-time partners, Theodore Bernardi and Donn Emmons, were very supportive and graciously gave their time to assist in the documentation of their relationship over their many years with Wurster.

We are thankful for the unfailing enthusiasm of Sarah (Sadie) Super, Wurster's daughter, and we are so glad that we can now share the story of her "Pops."

Very grateful thanks to those important people who have helped the subject to come alive through their time, association, experiences, and personal contact with Wurster: Elizabeth Church, Ella Hagar, Donald B. Rice Jr., Frances Comstock, Lois Langhorst, Edward Barnett, Professor Kenneth Cardwell, Professor Harold Stump, Joshua Baer, Van Maren King, Professor Donlyn Lyndon, Rudolph Peterson, Professor Roselyn Lindheim, Professor Howard Friedman, Arthur Waugh, Professor Henry Lagorio, Kellam deForest, Professor Joseph Esherick, and George Homsey.

For the last twenty years, The Environmental Design Archives at the College of Environmental Design at the University of California, Berkeley, has provided access to much of the design material of not only the Bay Area architects, but also work from around the world. The Archives were established by Professor Kenneth Cardwell in 1958 and with minimal funding and much hard work, the dedicated staff has systematically catalogued mountains of files, data, and images into what is now considered one of the premier architectural design archives in the world. The William Wurster Collection, which also includes the Catherine and William Wurster collection is one of the most extensive collections in the archive. This facility, and the authors, are especially indebted to the work of the curator Waverly Lowell and the faculty curators Professor Stephen Tobriner and Professor Marc Treib; their dedication has created this very valuable resource. The archives catalogued and preserved the documents that Dick salvaged from the Wurster offices and then expanded this collection with holdings from the offices after World War II, and most recently with that acquisition of the Catherine and William Wurster Collection. The assistant curators Carrie McDade and Miranda Hambro gave generously of their time and equally of their enthusiasm.

Because of her longstanding interest and knowledge of Bay Area architecture, Elizabeth Kendall Thompson's readings of our manuscript gave clarity and breadth to the writing.

Many friends and colleagues provided support and encouragement. We are indebted to Professor Charles W. Moore, Professor Ernesto Rogers, Donald B. Rice Jr., Professor David Gebhard, William Turnbull, and Professor

Lawrence B. Anderson for their comments and critiques.

Sally Woodbridge and William Coburn, both very knowledgeable about Wurster's architecture, have facilitated awareness of Wurster's work, and we are grateful for their contributions over these years, and for their assistance with the preparation of this volume.

During the early years of this project, Daniel Gregory and Jeffrey Chusid, two graduate students at Berkeley who are now gifted architectural historians, ably assisted Professor Peters in the initial primary research. Thank you.

For their periodic council, time, and expertise, we thank William Stout, Keith and Jessica Wilson, Professor and Dean Jennifer Wolch, Michael Carabetta, Elizabeth Byrne, Jennifer Lovett, Gay Falk, Dianne Harris, Alison Brantley, Madeline Johnston, Susan Lehmann, and Bob Beck.

We are so appreciative of the generosity of the many homeowners, who in the sharing of their personal stories, brought the architecture even more clearly into view: Deliah Fleishaker Erlich, Paolo and Sharon Lee Polledri, Dr. and Mrs. Howard Maibach, Kathe Hardy, Hal and Mary Jo Feeney, Helene F. Belz , Mr. and Mrs. Avrum Gratch, Summer Smith, Frank Birchfield and Sarah Harpham, Judy Houteling, Bernard and Ruth Issenman, Patricia Pope, Peter and Midge Zischke, Andrew Dreyfus and Diane Harwood, Roselyn Chroman Swig, and the many others who prefer to remain anonymous

Thankfully, E.M. Ginger took our almost-complete text and pulled together all of the loose ends and asked all of the critical questions that gave us the key to completion. Before that, and for the same reasons, we are indebted to the help and support of Sylvia Russell.

We are so pleased that the best publisher of architectural books in America wanted to pursue and publish this book. Princeton Architectural Press has been a joy to work with. We couldn't have asked for a better outcome. Specifically we enjoyed the encouragement and criticism of our editor Dan Simon, as well as that of Clare Jacobson and Laurie Manfra.

Without the incredible and unfailing support of our families this would have been impossible. With love and thanks to our partners in life. For Richard Peters to Donald Rice. For Caitlin Lempres Brostrom to Nathan Brostrom and Matthew Lempres and their children: Mary, David, Ellen, Wally, Sarah, and Anna.

Primary Professional Collaborators

Morley Baer (1916–1995)

Architectural photography was extremely important to Morley Baer. Although he was renowned for his evocative photographs of the Monterey Peninsula in California and for his work in many books regarding its landscape and buildings, his interest was not in the picturesque beauty of nature but rather in the role of what people did to, and in, it. Architecture was the most obvious example of this and the bulk of his work examined the relationships among building, man, and landscape. His photographs made buildings look strong and real without sterilizing or commercializing the image—architects loved this reality and his career blossomed after he started portraying Wurster's work in the 1940s.

Born in 1916 and raised in Toledo, Ohio, Baer first came to California in 1939 in search of the photographer Edward Weston. Baer received a master's degree in literature from the University of Michigan and served in the U.S. Navy during World War II. Following the war, he resumed his personal passion for photography and in 1946 returned to the Monterey Peninsula and opened a small studio in Carmel focusing on the standard fare of portraits and weddings.

In the late 1940s Baer and his wife, Frances, moved to the San Francisco Bay Area. After ten years of successful work with Wurster's office (Wurster, Bernardi & Emmons) and then also with Skidmore, Owings & Merrill, Baer bought the Wursters' house, designed by Rudolf Schindler, on Greenwood Commons. The Wursters and Baers then became social as well as professional friends.

Baer returned full time to the Monterey Peninsula in 1965, after Wurster completed a stone house for him at Garapota Creek near Big Sur. From his base in California, Baer photographed the natural and man-made landscape for over fifty years. He was a recipient of the American Institute of Architects' gold medal for photography and a Prix de Rome fellowship from the American Academy in Rome.[1]

Theodore Bernardi (1903–1990)

Theodore Bernardi was born in 1903 in Yugoslavia and emigrated in 1912 to Oakland, California, when he was nine years old. In 1924, Bernardi graduated from the University of California, Berkeley, with a degree in architecture. Bernardi apprenticed in several Bay Area architectural firms and also worked on a WPA-funded project documenting historically significant architecture in California (HABS projects).

After working on the art deco Fox Theater with Timothy Pflueger in Oakland, Bernardi joined Wurster's office in 1930, becoming Wurster's fourth staff person. When Wurster moved east in the early 1940s, Bernardi started a new practice. However, by 1944, Wurster and Bernardi (while Wurster was living on the East Coast) had established a partnership. A year later, in 1945, they asked Donn Emmons to join them.

Bernardi taught at the University of California, Berkeley, as a lecturer and continued to work with Wurster, Bernardi & Emmons.

At the time of his death, it was said of Bernardi that: "Theodore's buildings were a reflection of himself: humble, a bit reticent, approachable, friendly, and above all, unpretentious, the latter characteristic quite remarkable, given the degree of his professional renown and the luster of his many awards."[2] This included the AIA architecture firm award In 1965.

Thomas Church (1902–1978)

Thomas "Tommy" Dolliver Church was born in Boston in 1902 and raised in Oakland, California. He received a degree in landscape architecture from the University of California, Berkeley, in 1922 and a master's degree in landscape design from Harvard University's Gradaute School of Design. While at Berkeley, he and Lockwood deForest studied together and became friends with William Wurster. While deForest moved back to Santa Barbara, Church stayed in the Bay Area and taught at Berkeley after the completion of his master's degree.

In 1930 Church was asked by Marion Hollins (with the encouragement of William Wurster) to assist in the development of a new golf course community in the Santa Cruz Mountains, Pasatiempo. In exchange for helping members whose new vacation homes had gardens, she built him a house designed by Wurster. Simultaneous to the establishment of this commission, Church opened offices in both Pasatiempo (in his home) and in San Francisco.

Church and Wurster maintained a close friendship and traveled together with Church's wife, Elizabeth (Betsy), to Europe in 1937. The highlight of this trip was the time they all spent with Alvar Aalto and his wife, Aino. Church's European travels greatly influenced his work, and he began to adopt a more abstract approach to landscape.

Church is credited with opening the door to the modern movement in landscape architecture, developing an approach that became known as the "California Style." Church published *Gardens are for People* in 1955, in which he stated the four principles for his design process: one, unity of house and garden; two, function relations of practical needs to decorative desires; three, simplicity upon which economic and aesthetic success lies; and four, scale the relation of parts to each other. These principles were often executed in the outdoor rooms he created as both counterpoint and support of the architecture.

As with Wurster and all of his collaborators, Church's work affected many of the landscape architects of the next generation; although educated in California, they practiced internationally,

most notably Lawrence Halprin and Garrett Eckbo. Church retired in 1977.

Lockwood deForest III (1896–1949)

Lockwood deForest III was a landscape architect based in Santa Barbara, California. Together with his wife, Elizabeth Kellam deForest, they established much of the tone of landscape design in California in the early 1920s. The deForests designed with spare and simple forms, emphasizing in their design the visual and functional relationships between indoors and out. They worked primarily with plants appropriate to the environment and native landscape. This allowed for a graceful transition to the critical distant views and, as importantly, created gardens that were easy to maintain. Their gardens influenced the next wave of West Coast innovation in landscape design, including Thomas Church.[3]

DeForest, born in 1896, was the son of the famed turn-of-the century painter of the same name. Since he was seven years old, his family, like many other well-to-do easterners, traveled west to Santa Barbara during the winter months in search of adventure and a better climate.

DeForest was educated at several universities including a year at the University of California, Berkeley in 1919; he met Wurster there, and then Thomas Church. DeForest collaborated on more than ten projects with Wurster. The Wurster office files include numerous letters between Wurster, Church, and deForest as they advised each other on various elements of their mutual projects.

DeForest developed an aesthetic that used regional inspirations as a source, coupled with an interest in abstract form and a taste for drama. He relied on the framed view as an organizing force. While this alone was not unusual for the time, his approach was because he emphasized the abstract as well as the pictorial qualities of a scene.

Donn Emmons (1910–1997)

Donn Emmons, Wurster and Theodore Bernardi's partner after 1945 and before that a staff architect since 1938, was a big man in size and presence. He was good-natured, a little reticent, and level-headed with an open mind. He listened carefully in meetings, participated in a hands-on way in discussing project details, and made decisions or gave directions as the situation required. While his focus was primarily architectural design, he also had a very good business sense, which his clients appreciated. He liked to sketch while talking, and was a perpetual doodler. While discussing designs with clients and colleagues around the conference table, he would be constantly sketching with his pen of choice, a Pentel felt-tip. He encouraged his junior staff as he looked for fresh solutions to problems and was always willing to try new ideas and take risks.[4]

Donn Emmons was born in New York, and studied architecture at Cornell University, graduating in 1933. Emmons came to California for a year of continued architectural education at the University of Southern California, and stayed in Los Angeles working in several architectural firms toward his licensing. These were the years of the Depression and work opportunities were limited. Having seen and appreciated Wurster's published works, Emmons traveled to San Francisco. Wurster's firm was one of the few thriving practices, and Emmons started to work there in 1938.

Emmons's success in the firm was clear when Wurster and Bernardi asked Emmons to join their partnership. During this time, and until Wurster's return to California in 1949, the continued success and development of the practice was due to the efforts of Bernardi and Emmons, who was involved in all aspects of running the office and the architectural work. He practiced architecture at the offices of Wurster, Bernardi & Emmons until he retired in 1985.

Lawrence Halprin (1916–2009)

Lawrence "Larry" Halprin, world-renowned landscape architect, recognized that "the garden in your own immediate neighborhood, preferably at your own doorstep, is the most significant garden," and as part of a seamless whole, he valued "wilderness areas where we can be truly alone with ourselves and where nature can be sensed as the primeval source of life."[5] The interplay of perspectives informed projects, which encompassed urban parks, plazas, commercial and cultural centers, and other places of congregation.

Lawrence Halprin was born in Brooklyn, New York, in 1916. Halprin studied horticulture and received his bachelor's degree from Cornell University in 1939 and a master's degree from the University of Wisconsin. Immediately after, he attended Harvard University's Graduate School of Design where he studied with Walter Gropius and Marcel Breuer—about the same time that Wurster was at Harvard, then Yale, then MIT. Halprin received a degree in landscape architecture from Harvard in 1943. A commissioned officer during World War II, he then settled in San Francisco, where he worked for Thomas Church from 1946 to 1948. He opened his own office in 1949, which became Lawrence Halprin and Associates in 1972.

Halprin's many award-winning projects include the Ghirardelli Square in San Francisco, and Greenwood Commons in Berkeley, with which he worked with Wurster. Some of his most critically acclaimed projects include the Franklin Delano Roosevelt Memorial in Washington D.C., The Sea Ranch Development in Northern California, and the Yosemite Falls Restoration in Yosemite Park, California. He received many awards and honors in his lifetime and one of the most distinguished was the Gold Medal from the American Institute of Architects in 1979. His career was legendary and he will always be celebrated as a man of passion and conviction about environmental conservation.

Roger Sturtevant (1903–1982)

Roger Sturtevant was born in 1903 in Alameda, California, a suburb on the east side of the San Francisco Bay. His photographic training was acquired informally through work in a camera shop and later in Dorothea Lange's studio. Encouraged by Lange, Edward Weston, and Imogen Cunningham, Sturtevant opened a studio in 1921.

Sturtevant's practice initially focused on abstract compositions and portraits, but with a commission in 1925 from *Pacific Coast Architect* to photograph a project by architect Bernard Maybeck, Sturtevant's architectural focus began to dominate his professional life. Sturtevant mostly shot the architecture of the West Coast. He had a notable concern for characteristics of the site, requirements of the owner, and integration of the interior and the exterior. He played a significant role in bringing the work of West Coast architects to national and international audiences.

William Wurster and Roger Sturtevant's first collaboration was with the Warren and Sarah Gregory House built in 1927, which won national attention after receiving the prestigious *House Beautiful* prize. They worked closely together throughout the rest of their careers. Roger Sturtevant retired in 1972.[6]

In 1982, Donn Emmons commented that Sturtevant:

had developed his own special approach to architectural photography to tell a complete story of a house, its character and setting and important details. These he would send to editors along with his own description of the project. The freshness of the house designs and the gardens, unlike anything being done in the East, intrigued the editors of *Architectural Forum*, *Pencil Points* and the *Record*, and virtually everything completed by the office was published by one or the other of them. Ultimately and inevitably this was labeled the Bay Area Style.[7]

The success of Wurster's work is undoubtly tied to Sturtevant's. As with all of Wurster's professional collaborators, their relationship was based both on a deep personal friendship and on great professional respect and trust.

Notes

PREFACE

1 William Wurster, "The Twentieth Century Architect," written for the committee on education, American Institute of Architects, 1948.

INTRODUCTION

1 William Wurster, "The Twentieth Century Architect," written for the committee on education, American Institute of Architects, 1948.
2 "Design in Practice: A Talk before the Ann Arbor Conference," Feb 3, 1945. William Wilson Wurster (WWW) personal notes, in collection of authors, 6.
3 Wurster's grandmother Anna was widowed when his father was young. She later remarried to Charles Albert Leopold Grunsky, a man of pioneer stock and father of eight. Wurster grew up among the Grunskys, a prosperous and cultured family that was influential in the community. His sister Helen later married into the architecturally inclined, Berkeley-based Maybeck family. Members of his large extended family helped establish Wurster's career, obtaining several commissions for the young architect, including his earliest—the design and construction of a house in Sacramento, California's state capitol, for his cousin Carroll Grunsky.
4 William Wilson Wurster, College of Environmental Design, University of California, Campus Planning, and Architectural Practice, an oral history conducted in 1964, Regional Oral History Office, The Bancroft Library, University of California, Berkeley, 4.
5 "William Wilson Wurster: College of Environmental Design, University of California, Campus Planning, and Architectural Practice," interview conducted by Suzanne B. Riess (Berkeley, CA: University of California Regional Cultural History Project, 1964), 15.
6 Oral history, 12.
7 Edward L. Barnett, interview by Richard C. Peters (RCP), ca. 1966.
8 Ibid., 53.
9 Diaries of William Wurster, 1923–24, Environmental Design Archives (EDA).
10 Ibid.
11 Ibid.
12 Ebenezer Howard, *Garden Cities of Tomorrow* (London: S. Sonnenschein & Co., 1902).
13 Letter, William Adams Delano to William Wurster. Wurster collection, EDA.

14 Letter, Marion Hollins to Wurster, November 1, 1928, EDA file III.520 "Pasatiempo Country Club."
15 WWW, office files, n.d., EDA III.339.
16 Similar in concept to Pasatiempo was the 1939 alpine winter resort Sugar Bowl in Soda Springs, California. A group of Wurster's former clients and friends, headed by master-skier Hans Shroll, engaged Wurster to design a lodge for the new ski resort. It was to be both a social center for a new collection of houses at the resort and a hotel for guests. Wurster said that the lodge was to be a "frame for the life of skiing " Wurster also designed several small cabins. The most notable of his commissions at the resort was the stone house he designed for the noted art collector, Jerome Hill.
17 "William Wilson Wurster," 92.
18 Ibid., 94.
19 The College of Environmental Design at Berkeley is housed in Wurster Hall, named in 1963 for both Catherine and William Wurster when he retired as dean.
20 Peter Oberlander and Eva Newbrun, *Houser: The Life and Work of Catherine Bauer* (Vancouver, BC: University of British Columbia Press, 1999).
21 Oral history, 105.
22 William Wurster, notes for lecture at Ann Arbor Conference, February 3, 1945, in collection of the authors.
23 "William Wilson Wurster," 119.
24 Oral history, 143.
25 William Wurster, "The University and the Environmental Design Professions," lecture at University of California, Berkeley, October 1959.
26 "William Wilson Wurster," 169.
27 Ibid., 174.
28 William Wurster, an interview with Wurster on the occasion of his retirement, *San Francisco Chronicle*, June 3, 1963, 11.
29 "William Wilson Wurster," 143.
30 Wurster, "The University and the Environmental Design Professions."
31 Ibid.
32 Ibid.
33 "William Wilson Wurster," 174.
34 Lawrence Anderson and Henry Russell Hitchcock, *Bulletin* (Cambridge, MA: Massachusetts Institute of Technology, 1950).
35 Wurster, Bernardi & Emmons's larger projects were the result of successful collaborations. In the case of the CASBS, Wurster's design was

integrally related to to the work of Thomas Church. At the Golden Gateways, they collaborated with Anshen and Allen, DeMars and Raey, Skidmore Owings & Merrill, and Warnecke and Associates. Ghiradelli Square was designed in collaboration with Lawrence Halprin. Bank of America's Headquarters was closely linked to efforts by Pietro Belluschi and Skidmore, Owings & Merrill, as well as Lawrence Halprin.

THE EARLY YEARS

1 Letter, WWW to Mrs. Smith, January 26, 1927, EDA Smith III.634.
2 Letter, WWW to Walter Reilly, March 19, 1929, EDA Smith III.634.
3 WWW essay, "Farmhouse for Mrs. Warren Gregory," n.d., EDA W.Gregory III.276.
4 WWW description, n.d., EDA W.Gregory III.276.
5 Letter, WWW to Charles Grunsky, January 14, 1942, EDA III.276.
6 Sally Woodbridge, *Bay Area Houses* (Salt Lake City, UT: Peregrine Smith Books, 1988), 157.
7 Letter, WWW to Sarah Gregory, n.d., EDA III.276.
8 Letter, Hagar to WWW, n.d., EDA Hagar III.291.
9 EH, conversation with Caitlin Lempres Brostrom (CLB), 1992.
10 Fifteen years later, during World War II, while Wurster was Dean at MIT, he designed a sleeping porch for the family. It was sheathed in plywood in large part because of the restricted availability of building materials, but also because both the client and architect's desire to have the design as straightforward and unembellished as possible. The sleeping porch has since been renovated and redetailed by the architect Mark Mack.
11 Office files, n.d., EDA IIIs.339.
12 *California Arts and Architecture*, reprint, June 1931, 7.
13 Letter, WWW to Marion Hollins, September 6, 1930: 1. EDA III.339.
14 Ibid., 2.
15 Originally built for Robert Howes, by completion of the project the manager had changed to Earl Kaplansky.
16 *Arts and Architecture*, reprint, June 1931, 7.
17 Description for publication in journals from WWW office, n.d., EDA Kaplansky, III.367.
18 While other early Wurster projects used redwood boards for the interiors (Gillespie, Gregory), this was the first where he mixed the

palette of materials in order to maintain the clarity of architectural intent. His house for the Pope family in Madera in 1956 is a clear link to this early system.

19 As Wurster's career developed, he continued to prioritize doorways by increasing or decreasing the scale and details of the doors and their casings.

20 Letter, WWW to Howes, February 10, 1930, EDA Kaplansky III.367.

21 Ibid.

22 Wurster used 3-foot-long "barn" shingles.

23 Early on, the family made this house a year-round residence and the screened bedrooms no longer made sense.

24 The house later became known as the Field/Wagner house.

25 Wurster later made an addition for Sally Field and Mattie Wagner by adding a high-vaulted living room and turning the original living room into the house's dining room. The original second-floor master bedroom and balcony were incorporated to look down into the new living room. A tall window at the end of the living room brought in generous daylight and, as well, allowed for continual balanced natural light in the second-floor bedroom.

26 Description for publication, n.d., EDA Church III.125.

27 Ibid.

28 "Homes Recall Simplicity of Mission Days: California Tradition Preserved in Architecture at Pasatiempo," *San Francisco Chronicle*, June 4, 1932, 7.

29 William Wurster, "Four Houses in California," *Architectural Record* 64, May 1936, 35.

30 WWW to Voss, October 21, 1931: 1. EDA Voss III.718.

31 WWW to Rudolf Mock at the New York Museum of Modern Art. July 7, 1938: 1. EDA Voss III.718.

32 WWW to Voss, 2.

33 Ibid.

34 Letter, WWW to James Lawrence, Jr., April 22, 1940. EDA Voss III.718.

MIDDLE PHASE

1 Letter, WWW to Benners, December 23, 1932, EDA Benner, Berkeley.III.45.

2 Letter, WWW to Delano, n.d, EDA Benner, Berkeley.III.45.

3 Demolished in the 1980s, a new house was built on the same site.

4 Description of house for possible publication, n.d., EDA Butler, Vincent. III.99.

5 Nora Kenyon was a well-known interior decorator who worked with Wurster on several projects. The apartments were built by GPW Jensen and Sons, who also built many of Wurster's houses.

6 Kathi Hardy, daughter, interview with CLB, June 18, 2010.

7 Ibid.

8 Statement for publication/promotional purposes, n.d., EDA WWW III.462.

9 Ibid.

10 Underdown blocks were called such because they were first developed in Australia. They were an early alternative to the contemporary concrete concrete-block building unit. They represented a new building technology and were manufactured locally. Hollow 10-by-10-inch brick floor tiles were used by Wurster in many projects because it was thought that the cavity reduced the possibility of dampness when placed on a slab on grade.

11 Interior designer Vera Christie worked with Wurster throughout his career—she had initially recommended him to the Wrights in the early 1920s for what he called "his first project." Letter, WWW to Vera Christie, August 14, 1936, EDA WWW files III.357.

12 WWW office description, n.d., EDA Jensen III.357.

13 There was also the intention of building a rental apartment on the lower portion of the site and views over this would have been essential as well.

14 WWW, description in office files, EDA Hamill III.294.

15 Ibid.

16 Project description, EDA Mendenhall III.454.

17 WWW, statement in office files, EDA Mendenhall III.454.

18 WWW, statement in office files, EDA Mendenhall III.454.

19 John Glogg, writer in London, England, preparing a book on rural architecture, February 17, 1938, EDA III.128.

20 Letter, WWW to Clark, April 12, 1937, EDA files III.128.

21 WWW, description in office files, EDA III.128

22 WWW, description in office files, EDA III.128

23 Letter, WWW to Architectural League of New York, EDA files III.273.

24 Ibid.

25 WWW, office files. EDA Green III.273.

26 Ibid.

THE LATE ERA

1 A remodel of the house and gardens was completed in 2007 by the architect Hugo Sap (Atelier Sap) and the landscape architects Silvina and Eric Blasen (Blasen Gardens).

2 *Architectural Forum*, July 1943, 52–53.

3 WWW, description, EDA Grover file III.284.

4 Ibid.

5 Ibid.

6 Ibid.

7 Ibid.

8 WWW, office files, EDA III.122.

9 Letter, Saxton Pope to WWW, November 4, 1939, EDA WWW Pope, Saxton III.543.

10 Ibid.

11 Ibid.

12 Ibid.

13 Ibid.

14 Ibid.

15 This was the last house where Wurster used underdown block. The Popes were not happy with the quality of the concrete they were made from.

16 Letter, Saxton Pope, November 4, 1939.

17 This house was later demolished when a freeway was built to connect rapidly developed suburban communities in this area. The Popes had Wurster design a home for them in Burlingame in 1933. Letter, Saxton Pope to WWW, November 16, 1939, EDA WWW Pope, Saxton III.543.

18 Letter, Saxton Pope to WWW, November 16, 1939, EDA WWW Pope, Saxton III.543.

19 Project description, EDA Walters III.1479.

20 Letter, WWW to Gwen Hodges, House and Home, December 30, 1952: 1. EDA Heller IV.687.

21 Ibid.

22 This house was reconstructed and entirely changed.

23 Patricia Pope, Wurster client, in interview with CLB, June 7, 2010.

24 The family had extensive timber interests and all the wood for the house came from their holdings—including the curving stair, which was made from one walnut tree.

25 "Two Houses: A Formal House in an Informal Setting," *Architectural Record* 127, no. 4 (April 1960), 190.

26 Joshua Baer, Baer's son, interview by CLB, July 27, 2010. Reflections on Wurster's description of project.

27 Ibid.

28 Ibid.

COLLABORATORS

1 All of the above from an interview by CLB with Joshua Baer, July 29, 2010, and Morley Baer's C.V.

2 In Memoriam, Gary R. Brown, Henry J. Lagorio, Harold A. Stump, University of California, Berkeley, 1994.

3 Robin Karsson, *A Genius for Place: American Landscapes of the Country Place Era* (Amherst, MA: University of Massachusetts, 2007), 283.

4 Van Maren King, reflections of WBE designer in 1964 and 1965, July 29, 2010.

5 Peter Walker and Melanie Simo, *Invisible Gardens: The Search for Modernism in the American Landscape* (Cambridge, MA: MIT Press, 1994), 9.

6 Oakland Art Museum of California, biographical statement.

7 Donn Emmons, from introductory comments to Bill Coburn's slideshow at the opening the Wurster Exhibit at AIA headquarters, August 11, 1982, 1–2, EDA.

Selected Bibliography

Publications

Bauer, Catherine. *Modern Housing*. Boston: Houghton Mifflin, 1934.

Church, Thomas. *Gardens Are For People*. New York: Reinhold, 1955.

Contemporary Architecture. San Francisco: San Francisco Museum of Art, 1937.

Creighton, Thomas, and Katherine Morrow Ford. *Contemporary Houses Evaluated by Their Owners*. New York: Reinhold, 1961.

Domestic Architecture of the San Francisco Bay Region. San Francisco: San Francisco Museum of Modern Art, 1949.

Hille, R. Thomas. *Inside the Large Small House: The Residential Design Legacy of William W. Wurster*. Princeton, NJ: Princeton Architectural Press 1994.

Hise, Greg. "The Roots of the Postwar Urban Region: Mass Housing and Community Planning in California, 1920–1950." Ph.D. dissertation, University of California, Berkeley 1992.

Hitchcock, Henry-Russell, and Arthur Drexler. *Built in USE: Post-war Architecture*. New York: Simon & Schuster, 1953.

Howard, Ebenezer. *The Garden Cities of Tomorrow*. London: Faber & Faber, 1902.

Karson, Robin. *A Genius for Place: American Landscapes of the Country Place Era*. Amherst, MA: University of Massachusetts, 2007.

Keeler, Charles. *The Simple Home*. Santa Barbara, CA: Peregrine Smith, 1904.

Longstreth, Richard. *On the Edge of the World: Four Architects in San Francisco at the Turn of the Century*. New York: Architectural History Foundation, 1983.

Lowell, Waverly. *Living Modern: A Biography of Greenwood Common*. Richmond, CA: William Stout Publishers, 2009.

Lowell, Waverly, Elizabeth Byrne, and Betsy Frederick-Rothwell, eds. *Design on the Edge: A Century of Teaching Architecture at the University of California, Berkeley, 1903–2003*. Berkeley, CA: College of Environmental Design, University of California, Berkeley.

Oberlander, Peter and Eva Newbrun. *Houser: The Life and Work of Catherine Bauer*. Vancouver, B.C.: University of British Columbia Press, 1999.

Partridge, Loren W. *John Galen Howard and the Berkeley Campus: Beaux Arts Architecture in the "Athens of the West."* Berkeley, CA: Berkeley Architectural Heritage Association, 1978.

Richards, J.M., and Elizabeth Mock. *Introduction to Modern Architecture*. Revised American edition. New York: Penguin Books, 1947.

Schildt, Goran. *Alvar Aalto: The Mature Years*. New York: Rizzoli International, 1991.

Scully, Vincent. *American Architecture and Urbanism*. New York: Praeger, 1969.

Telesis Environmental Research Group. *Space for Living*. San Francisco: San Francisco Museum of Modern Art, 1940.

Treib, Marc, ed. *An Everyday Modernism: The Houses of William Wurster*. Berkeley, Los Angeles and London: San Francisco Museum of Modern Art, University of California Press. 1995.

"William Wilson Wurster: College of Environmental Design, University of California, Campus Planning, and Architectural Practice." 2 vols. Interview by Suzanne B. Reiss. Berkeley, CA: University of California, Regional Cultural History Project (now Regional Oral History Office), 1964.

Woodbridge, Sally, ed. *Bay Area Houses*. Salt Lake City, UT: Peregrine Smith, 1988.

Wurster, William Wilson. "The Twentieth-Century Architect." In *Architecture—A Profession and a Career*. Washington D.C.: American Institute of Architects Press, 1945.

Articles

"The Center for Advanced Study in the Behavioral Sciences." *Arts and Architecture* 71, no. 2 (February 1955): 34–41.

Church, Elizabeth. "Pasatiempo." *California Arts and Architecture* 39 (June 1931): 40–42.

"Contemporary Juxtapositions: Robert Hering Makes a 1951 William Wurster House His Own." *Interior Design* 51 (1980): 254–57.

Esherick, Joseph. "Image and Reality." *Places* 7, no 1 (Fall 1990): 86.

Gregory, Daniel P. "An Indigenous Thing: The Story of William Wurster and the Gregory Farmhouse." *Places* 7, no. 1 (Fall 1990): 78–93.

Hamlin, Talbot Faulkner. "What Makes It American: American Architecture of the Southwest and the West." *Pencil Points* 20 (December 1939): 774–75.

———. "Of Houses as Places to Live." *Pencil Points* 19, no. 8 (August 1938): 487–89.

"A Minimum House by William Wilson Wurster." *Pencil Points* 26 (1945): 70–72.

Mumford, Lewis. "The Sky Line: The Status Quo." *The New Yorker.* 23 (October 1947): 107–09.

Peters, Richard. "L'architetto William Wurster." *Casabella continuita*, no. 238 (April 9, 1960): 60–73.

"Portrait." *Architectural Forum* 102 (1955): 85.

"3 Houses Built for Summer." *House and Garden* 137 (1970): 86–95.

"West Coast Architect William Wilson Wurster." *Arts and Architecture* 81 (1964): 20–55.

"William Wilson Wurster to Receive A.I.A. 1969 Gold Medal." *Architectural Record* 145 (1969): 36.

Wurster, William Wilson. "L'Architettura moderna on California." *Casabella continuita*, no. 238 (9 April 1960): 13.

———. "Architectural Education." *AIA Journal* 9, no. 1. (January 1948): 36.

———. "From the Log Cabin to Modern House: An Architect Urges a Return to Simple Fundamentals in Planning Our New Homes." *New York Times Magazine*, January 20, 1946.

———. "Tell Me, What Is Modern Architecture?" *House and Garden* 77, no. 4 (April 1940): 46–47, 71; *House and Garden* 77, no. 5 (May 1940): 50, 60.

———. "Toward Urban Redevelopment." *Architect and Engineer* (July 1944): 25–28.

———. 25 Most Important Houses in America." *Fine Homebuilding* 179 (2006): 58–67. Special feature in the annual "Houses" issue on the 25th anniversary of *Fine Homebuilding*.

———. "When Is a Small House Large?" *House and Garden* 92, no. 2 (August 1947): 72–75.

Record of Publication

(for projects described in book)

**Bank of America Headquarters,
San Francisco, California**
Architectural Review, January 1964, pp. 128–29
Baumeister, March 1971, pp. 262–67
AIA Journal, August 1980, pp. 49–55

Benner House, Berkeley, California
Architectural Forum, May 1936, pp. 394–401
House Beautiful, May 1936, pp. 94–95
Modern Bauformen, November 1936, pp. 614–61
Architettura, January 1940, p. 56
Sunset, July 1940, p. 18
Architectural Forum, October 1940, p. 253

**Butler House, Pasatiempo, Santa Cruz,
California**
American Architect, May 1937, p. 46
Pencil Points, August 1938, pp. 476–77
California (California Chamber of Commerce
  Magazine) March 1939, p. 10
House Beautiful, September 1940, pp. 86–87
Sunset, April 1941, pp. 16–17

**Center for Advanced Study of Behavioral
Science, Stanford University**
Arts and Architecture, February 1955, pp. 14–16
Architecture d'aujourd'hui, October 1956, pp. 42–43
Domus, April 1957, pp. 3–6

Chase Grover House, San Francisco, California
California Arts and Architecture, December 1940,
  pp. 28–29

**Church House, Pasatiempo, Santa Cruz,
California**
California Arts and Architecture, June 1931, p. 42
California Arts and Architecture, July–August 1932,
  pp. 13, 23

Architectural Record, October 1934,
  pp. 229–33
Architectural Forum, October 1937, p. 262
Sunset, December 1937, p. 262
Home of the West, May 1938
Pencil Points, August 1938, p. 486
Redwood Association Bulletin, September
  1938, p. 15

Clark House, Aptos, California
Architectural Record, January 1938, p. 58
Architectural Forum, June 1938, pp. 507–09
House Beautiful, June 1938, pp. 27, 59
Pencil Points, June 1938
Sunset, June 1938, pp. 14, 38–39
Architect and Engineer, October 1938, p. 47
L'Architecture D'Aujoud'Hui, November 1938, p. 76
California (California Chamber of Commerce
  Magazine), March 1939, p. 11
Architectural Forum, October 1940, p. 241

Dondo House, Point Richmond, California
Architectural Record, December 1937, p. 69
Architectural Record, January 1938, p. 61
Architectural Record, March 1938, pp. 140–42
House Beautiful, March 1938, p. 54
Christian Science Monitor, July 2, 1940, p. 6

**George Pope House, El Peco Ranch,
Madera, California**
AIA Journal's Western Homes Awards, 1957, p. 4
Architectural Record, April 1960, pp. 193–96

**Golden Gateway Condominiums,
San Francisco, California**
Arts and Architecture, November 1960, pp. 18–19
Process: Architecture, October 1989, pp. 50–55

Green House, Walnut Creek, California
House Beautiful, February 1941, p. 27

W. Henderson House, Hillsborough, California
Architectural Record, April 1960, pp. 189–92
House and Garden, August 1961, pp. 68–73
House Beautiful, August 1963, pp. 68–71

Hollins House, Pasatiempo, California
California Arts and Architecture, June 1931, pp. 22, 40
House Beautiful, July 1932, pp. 16–17
Architectural Forum, October 1937, p. 270
The Key to Your New Home, 1938, p. 28
Pencil Points, August 1938, p. 471
Magazine of Sigma Chi, July 1939, p. 208
Architectural Forum, October 1941, p. 276

Mendenhall House, Palo Alto, California
Sunset, June 1938, p. 52
Architectural Record, March 1939, pp. 118–20

Miller House, Carmel, California
House Beautiful, March 1937, p. 48
Architectural Forum, October 1937, p. 296
The Key to Your New Home, 1938, pp. 62, 116
Pencil Points, August 1938, pp. 478–79
California Redwood Association Bulletin, September 1938, p. 13
Christian Science Monitor, January 1940, p. 6

Baer House, Big Sur, California
House and Garden, June 1970, pp. 86–95

S. Pope House, Orinda, California
House Beautiful, February 1941, pp. 18–29
House and Garden, August 1943, pp. 16–19
New Pencil Points, October 1943, pp. 74–77
California Arts and Architecture, December 1943, pp. 19–21
Ladies Home Journal, July 7, 1949, pp. 118–20

Sloss House, Woodside, California
Architectural Forum, October 1937, p. 297
Pencil Points, August 1938, p. 470

Voss House, Big Sur, California
Architectural Forum, May 1936, pp. 390–93
House Beautiful, July 1936, pp. 48–49
Moderne Bauformen, November 1936, pp. 618–62
Rob Wagner's *Script* back cover, December 23

W. Gregory House, Scott's Valley, California
House Beautiful, March 1931, p. 217
Architecture, August 1935, pp. 91–94
Pencil Points, August 1938, pp. 472–74
Places, October 1990, pp. 78–93

Walters House, San Francisco, California
House and Home, September 1952, pp. 134–39

Illustration Credits

Index